I0464398

Preparing to Manage Millions

How to Escape The Biggest Money Mistakes In College
And Set Yourself Up For A Life Of Prosperity

By Marcus L. Howard

This book is dedicated to my saving grace; the one who *freed me from my own mental enslavement.*

Bad Guy Notice:

We expect you to abide by these rules as we regularly search the internet for people who violate this copyright. Now that we have that out of the way, let's learn the powerful secrets of Financial Antermology and managing millions.

Acknowledgments

Writing a book is a process that is rarely done alone. Although there is usually one author, the number of people involved can be quite vast. I truly appreciate the army of people who believed in me and have told me that writing this book was possible.

I would like to thank my mother, Jeanette Oliver, for teaching me so many life lessons and allowing me the freedom to carve my own path in life. Thank you, Chelsea Irwin, for encouraging me to not only start but follow through with this great project. I would like to thank one of my greatest friends, David Tate, for listening and encouraging me throughout our lasting friendship. A big thank you to Tameka Washington for helping clear the clutter that kept me from my life's purpose. And thank you, Jodi Callender, for exhibiting patience and understanding when faced with the emotional highs and lows that went into finishing this very special project.

Finally, I wish to acknowledge my mentors who have helped me through the years in developing CoPocket, and shaping me into who I am today. Thank you, Mr. Eric Sivertsen, for your advice, guidance, and endless chai teas that you brought me during our many very helpful life discussions. Lastly, thank you, Professor Mike Ryan, for not only being a great mentor and professor, but for being a true friend.

Table of Contents

Introduction

"Academic qualifications are important and so is financial education. They're both important and schools are forgetting one of them." -Robert Kiyosaki

Imagine volunteering for an experiment in which the experimenter grants you the opportunity to walk out of the room and be financially set for the rest of your life. All you have to do is follow the rules they give you. If you don't follow them, there is a good chance you will leave the experiment miserable for a very long time.

You start the experiment with very little money and it is your task to create financial opportunities for yourself. In order to do this, you must ask a series of people you don't know for loans.

The people you borrow from make a living loaning money to you, your family and friends, as well as people you will never meet in your lifetime. For that reason, this experiment will not be easy because those lenders are very selective about who they give money to. You must prove to them that you have the ability to follow through on your promise to pay them what you owe...plus interest!

The amount of interest you will have to pay depends on whether or not you correctly follow the rules of the experiment. If you make the right decisions, you have to pay very little. If you make the wrong ones, you have to pay significantly more.

You are given a long list of complicated and, at times, contradicting rules. The top of the goal list reads:

"It is your objective to pay back your loans and leave the room with as much money as you can as quickly as you can. It is in your best interest to make the right decisions so that you can leave financially free when the experiment is over."

Those who loan you money will not care about extenuating circumstances or the fact that you may not fully understand the rules. If you are late with payments, you will leave the experiment with significantly less money.

There will be people throughout the experiment who will give you advice on how to proceed and what rules to follow. The problem is, very few are right. Some will confidently tell you things that will ruin your chances of walking away with any money at all. Others will give you sound advice that you should really use. Unfortunately for you, it will be really hard to tell the difference!

Right before you start, the experimenter leans over to your right ear and gives you this advice:

"Only a select few of the long list of rules are correct...it is your challenge to quickly figure out the correct ones on your own!"

How would you feel if you had just volunteered for this experiment? Here's a secret:

This isn't an experiment. It is your life!

It is what will happen to you when you start on your path toward financial independence. You will be bombarded with credit card offers, loan offers, and individuals who will lie to you and tell you that they are trying their hardest to give you free money.

Most of all, the offers that you will receive are going to be a scam in one way or another. Many of these scam companies (and some legitimate ones) feed off of the fact that you do not fully understand the penalties that you will pay if you don't play according to their ever-changing rules. It is how finance companies produce billions in revenue every year.

This experiment is almost impossible to pass and result in a significant amount of money in your pocket—and it will not be of any fault of your own. There are so many forces working against your success. Many talented people have tried and failed. The only way that you can leave the experiment with some significant cash is if you know the select set of rules to follow.

In real life, your financial success has very little to do with intelligence or income. Believe it or not, the most financially successful people are not always those who graduate top of their class or majored in accounting. So if it's not the extremely intelligent or the math majors who win the financial experiment, who does?

I'll tell you. The financial experiment is won by those who learn the correct rules and constantly reevaluate their strategies to stay ahead of the curve. It has nothing to do with how much you make, what school you attended, or how much money you have saved.

It is about a decision to master the game that determines how financially sound you will be for the rest of your life. It's about realizing that you have unlimited financial possibilities; it is a discipline called Financial Antermology.

Who Should Read This Book?

This book is designed for college students, but it is not beyond the scope of the high school junior or senior. If you are recently out of college and are looking for a book to jumpstart you on budgeting and building your credit, this is the perfect book for you.

> *Formal education will make you a living; self-education will make you a fortune!*
> *—Jim Rohn*

I say this because it is never too late to figure out how to manage your finances. The decisions you make just out of college are some of the most important decisions you will make in your lifetime. They are comparable to finding the right job, choosing a spouse, and buying your dream home.

Your financial decisions will follow you wherever you go and will have a large influence on the type of life that you live. So no matter how old you are and what stage of life you are in, the information in this book is important to you.

Why You Should Read This Book

I am almost positive that unless your parents are finance wizards, you have had very little education on financial management. You have been to school, and they taught you very useful information about

> *The problem is no one has taken the time to teach you the necessary knowledge that you need to have once you are out of college.*

philosophers, chemistry, economics, etc. I highly doubt that you have ever taken a class on Money Management 101. If you have, then you are light years ahead of about 98% percent of college students. If you aren't currently there, this book will make sure that you are.

How to win the financial experiment is just as important as any other subject that you will take in school. The problem is no one has taken the time to teach you the necessary knowledge that you need to have once you are out of college. They have not taught you how to properly manage your finances. Most students believe that managing their finances is easy enough and can be figured out without much help. This way of thinking is absolutely wrong! Everyone needs a little help, especially in unfamiliar arenas. There are people in the real world who earn a living by devising new ways to pull a fast one on those who do not know how to manage their money. Some of them are nothing more than loan sharks in nice suits trying to pass themselves off as legitimate business people looking out for your future.

Most people new to finance (and veterans for that matter) fall for these traps and find themselves in a world of trouble. I have made it my mission to help people overcome a system that is designed to make the most money while putting immense financial stress on you and the ones you love. It truly is not fair that they live stress-free lives, taking all of your hard-earned money while you constantly worry about how you are going to pay all your compounding bills on time.

You need to read this book so you can break free of the system like I did. You need to read this book so you can stop the system in its tracks and make it work for you. It is easier than you think; you just need to learn the system and make a commitment to yourself that you are going to do what it takes to secure your financial freedom.

The advice in this book will stay with you for the rest of

your life. After a short time, it should become second nature to you. Lucky for me, I took the time while in high school and college to learn the system; but I know countless others who were not so lucky. I want you to be ahead of the curve so that you can spend the bulk of your life wondering where you want to go on vacation and not where you are going to find the m money to finish paying off your credit cards!

This book debunks the myths and secrecy that stand between you and financial freedom. I highly doubt that this selfish system to extract money from citizens will change for the better any time soon, so I

Creditors automatically assume there is something wrong with you and that you don't know how to manage your money.

want you to know how to make it work in your own favor. You could learn the strategies and secrets to financial success like I did through years of trial and error, but I would not advise you to gamble with the rest of your life like I did!

This book shows you how to do it by sharing with you my experiences as well as my friends' while fully sharing with you the successful system I use in my life and with my clients every day.

A Quick Note on Those Uninterested In Your Future

When talking about finances, many people don't care whether you have the know-how to effectively manage your finances. They usually assume that you don't until you prove them otherwise. When it comes to finances, you are guilty until proven innocent.

"What does guilty mean," you ask? I will tell you my friend.

Guilty means that you are going to pay a high interest rate until you can prove to them that you will most certainly pay your bills on time. They mostly assume that you will not pay on time and will choose to offer you higher interest rates. This is not fair. Creditors automatically assume there is something wrong with you and you do not know how to manage your money.

I operate from the assumption that there is something wrong with the system and it should be changed. I don't think that there is anything wrong with you or that you are not worthy of a lower interest rate. What I do believe is that you are currently at a disadvantage. It is a creditor's job to keep you behind so that they can get ahead. And for that reason, there needs to be some changes made to the way you approach your finances.

I'll show you how your perception of finances affects not only how well you will live, but also how your parents, children, cousins, aunts, and uncles will live as a result of your newfound knowledge. Figuring out the financial puzzle is an indefinite boost to anyone's self-esteem.

This book lets you in on the secrets of Financial Antermologists. These people have completely paid off their student loans, do not have outstanding credit card debt, are living the life of their dreams, and they don't even make six figures! In order to get to this point, you will have to commit to learning the very basics of what Financial Antermologists know.

Even if you already know about investing, or about savings accounts and budget plans, you will not find a more comprehensive text on how to combine all the necessary knowledge to effectively ensure you financial future. In this book you will discover a plethora of practical tips and techniques on how to effectively budget, build your credit, and get your credit profile to work for you. This book includes:

- · The basics of budgeting and disciplined spending

- · What to do when you run into a financial emergency

- · How to make your own financial categories to live within **YOUR** means

- · How to decide what is more important when it is time to make difficult financial decisions

- · How to **save** money in college while affording all of the things that you need.

- · The fundamentals of credit

- · How to make your credit work for you

- · How to easily boost your credit score with a few simple adjustments

- · The top 10 mistakes people make when dealing with credit

- · How to win the credit card game

- · How loans will save your life!

Put plainly, I'll teach you how to play the financial game and win. Not only will I show you everything that you must do in order to be financially free, but I will also show you everything you should NOT do when moving toward your financial freedom. I'll go through the entire process with you and leave nothing to chance. I want this book to serve as the vehicle that will start you on the way to the life of your dreams.

Are you ready to get started? I know I am. Let's do it!

Part I- Budgeting

Chapter 1

How Much Does College Really Cost?

*"Talk may be cheap but intelligent conversation is very
expensive these days. Ask anyone with a kid in college."*
-Anonymous

A college education is a very large investment. Not only does this financial decision affect you immediately, it will affect the rest of your life as well. While both students and parents consider tuition costs when deciding on a college, many forget about the extra money that must be spent on books, phone bills, clothes, etc. A student on their own for the first time also may not realize just how soon and how often such bills add up.

Believe me, if you are not prepared with an effective budget, you will find yourself using your credit card to pay for your pizza!

In order to begin to budget efficiently, you must know and understand the difference between recurring, variable, and yearly expenses. Preparing for all expenses, instead of just immediate expenses, will take you a very long way on the road to your financial success in both college and in your professional life. Let's take a detailed look at each type of expense and how to prepare for them.

Recurring Expenses

Recurring expenses are expenses that must be paid down in thirty days or less. For a college student, examples of recurring expenses are car payments, phone bills, and credit card payments. When you start your professional life, you will incur additional recurring expenses like insurance payments, mortgage payments, etc. Depending on how well you wish to live, recurring expenses can be a small or very large part of your budget. Preparing yourself for recurring expenses is very simple. Here is what you have to do:

List your recurring expenses. You should know when they are due and the amount of each payment. At the beginning of each month, write down all of your expenses so that you know what must be paid down by the end of the month.

For example, let's say that you are an incoming freshman with a new car, cell phone, and two Visa credit cards. Lucky for you, your parents are making payments on the car but they tell you that you must pay your phone bill and credit cards on your own. You love to talk, so you have the unlimited plan that costs you $99 a month. On top of that, you have a recurring bill on both of your credit cards and the minimum payment for each is $52 a month. Your total monthly recurring expenses would be $202.

A part time job at your school will cover this payment. If you make $600 a month, it would, on average, consume about 35 percent of your monthly budget. I would leave an additional 10 percent in your recurring expense budget to cover any overage charges on your phone or extra items that you may have charged on your credit card.

At first glance, $202 a month does not sound like a big number. For a lot of people, it isn't. But you must also consider the fact that credit card payments and a phone bill are only a bare minimum of recurring expenses that students acquire. You may have other recurring expenses like a haircut, a cable bill, car insurance, or maybe a full-body seaweed wrap at the spa! These additional expenses means you will need to allocate about 70 – 80 percent of your monthly income on your recurring expenses.

If you are spending this much on your recurring expenses, you will not have enough money to save for your variable expenses and/or yearly expenses. This means that you will either have to do one of three things: Reduce your recurring expenses, find a better job, or find an alternate source of income to reduce your recurring expenses. If all else fails, you can make some of your recurring expenses variable expenses.

Variable Expenses

Variable expenses are expenses that have no set payment schedule. They are expenses that can come up on any different day or month. Variable expenses can be anything from restaurant bills, your books for the semester, clothes, etc. Variable expenses are not scheduled as recurring expenses, but there is some consistency in the amount that is usually spent over time.

Variable expenses are probably the trickiest expense to budget. Most people make the grave mistake of not budgeting variable expenses at all. Many new students feel that because these expenses seem random, that you honestly cannot budget them. This could not be any farther from the truth.

Here is how to budget for variable expenses.

There are many kinds of variable expenses. Some variable expenses should receive higher priority than others. For example, your college books are a variable expense that should take precedence over any other variable expense that you have. You enrolled in college to get the best education possible. You do not want to sell yourself short by not paying for your books because you had to have that perfect outfit.

Textbooks on average can cost anywhere from $200 to close to $600 per semester. If you feel that you will not have that much cash on hand, create a recurring savings account where you allocate a portion of your monthly pay check to pay for your books for the next semester. Think about it: how much easier would it be to put away $50 over 10 months instead of $500 in one month?

If you have a meal plan at your school, eating out is a variable expense that should not be placed high on the priority list. Sometimes, students make the mistake of eating out too often. If you do it, don't fret, it is not entirely your fault. Riddle me this: if your mom cooked meatloaf every day, it would not take long for you to get tired of meatloaf correct? The same applies to cafeteria food. If you eat the same type of meals long enough, you will crave something different.

The problem is that a lot of students spend too much money on eating out and it kills their budget. A great way to counter how much you spend on extra food is to balance what you eat at the cafeteria. If you are

Eating out once a week will give you a much needed break from cafeteria food.

allowed to create your own meals, be creative so that you do not eat the same type of meal too often. If you do not have a choice, try as many new things as you can (but stay away from the veal cobbler, though). This way, you can start to realistically reduce the times you eat out to once or maybe twice a week.

As for shopping, have a plan for how much you are willing to spend. You will be surprised how well you can spend the money that you allocate for shopping. You must realize that shopping malls are designed to get you to spend the most money you can on an impulse. It is your job to not fall victim to this trap and to take your time, strategize, and do not deviate too far from your original budget.

Variable expenses are expenses that should be managed the most carefully so allocate a sensible amount. It should be the last expense on your list that money should be allocated to. When calculating variable expenses, it is very important to keep in mind that you will also need money for your yearly expenses as well.

Yearly Expenses

Like the name states, yearly expenses are any expense that needs to be made on an annual basis. Yearly expenses are everything from tuition, vacations, and plane tickets home. They are usually the most expensive and have to be paid in one lump sum. Lucky for you, even though they are due in one lump sum, you do not need to come up with the money all at once. Here is a way to prepare for yearly expenses.

Tuition is a very large expense that usually requires an outside loan to finance. For that reason, your monthly income will not need to be used to pay down tuition. If you are a student who has to pay all or part of your tuition without loans, a summer job is almost absolutely necessary. With a summer job, a lot of that income can be saved to help with the larger tuition payment that must be made in August or September.

The goal is to not have to work full time while you are in school. If you do that, you are not doing your job, your schooling, or yourself any good. Working full time, no matter the job, can put a real strain on your educational experience. In order to prevent this from happening, a successful budget is essential. This means saving for your yearly expenses the entire year, not just a couple months before.

Conclusion

At the end of the day, it is truly important to sit down and think about how much college truly costs. While most look at the price of tuition, many don't think about the number of bills that they will have once they are in school. Hopefully, this chapter has provided some insight on what you have to budget for as you start taking control of your finances.

With ever-changing advances in technology, budgeting has become a lot easier and more efficient. There are a number of budgeting tools online that will automate everything that I have talked about in this chapter. For more details, all you have to do is go to my website www.copocket.co and look at the many resources available.

Next, I'll discuss the Top 10 financial mistakes that college students make while in school.

Review

1. Recurring expenses are bills that must be paid down in thirty days or less.

2. Make sure to figure out how much your bills are each month; this will determine the amount of money you need to break even for the month.

3. Variable expenses have no set payment schedule. They are expenses that can pop up on any different day or month.

4. Yearly expenses need to be made on an annual basis. Yearly expenses are everything from tuition, vacations, and plane tickets home.

5. Don't spend money until you have determined all of your expenses for the month or possibly the semester.

Review Questions

1. How soon do recurring expenses have to be repaid?

2. When is it appropriate to go over your spending limit while shopping?

3. How tasty is veal cobbler?

Chapter 2

Top 10 Mistakes College Students Make

*"The things taught in schools and colleges are not an
education, but the means to an education."*
- Ralph Waldo Emerson

How would you feel if you had a final exam on the first day of class? Not only that, but it accounts for a large part of your grade and it covers a large amount of material that the professor won't cover until deep into the semester. How well do you think you would do? If you think there is a good chance that you will fail, you are probably right!

To be fair, the professor decides you should have a second chance, and she needs more assignments to factor your grade, so she teaches the material during the semester and gives you periodic quizzes. With each quiz, you are given the opportunity to build on the grade that you got when you took the final.

Here you have a choice: You can either work really hard on the quizzes and still end up with a passing grade or you can give up hope and meander through the course. Which would you do? What do you think a Financial Antermologist would do? If you said the Financial Antermologist would work hard on the quizzes, you are wrong!

The Financial Antermologist would have researched the class beforehand. They would have either opted out of taking the class or found someone who took the class who could help them study. That way, once they aced the test on the first day, the rest of the course would be smooth sailing.

This Is A Lot Like Your Life After College!

Many students leave college without the basic knowledge they will need to efficiently manage their finances. Many do not know how to balance a budget or use a savings account, and lack even basic knowledge of investing. As a result, they are forced to learn them at the same time they are required to use them. It is a lot like our final exam scenario described above. To be honest, waiting until after graduation to learn these necessary tools is almost too late.

More importantly, learning these tools later rather than sooner will cost you money. Your credit card, auto loan, and mortgage rates will be much higher if you can get them at all. You will also be more prone to financial emergencies, which could potentially damage your credit and further hinder your financial success. If you are not prepared beforehand, you will have to work very hard just to stay in the race. Being immediately successful financially without learning the necessary skills is like maneuvering successfully through a stunt course without anyone ever teaching you how to drive. It is not going to happen!

To help prevent this, here is a list of the top ten mistakes that college students make during their years as a student and helpful tools on how to prevent them. This list covers both credit and budgeting mistakes. Hopefully you will gain the discipline to not make these mistakes yourself while you are in school. Read them carefully as it can save you tens, maybe hundreds of thousands of dollars, in interest charges during your life.

Top Ten Mistakes College Students Make While in School

1. Credit Card Debt

This is a common mistake that almost 90% of college students make within their first year of college: collecting credit cards. Did you know that the average student leaves college with about $2,700 in credit card (yes credit card) debt? This number is very good news to the banks but is very bad news to you. With college students receiving an average annual interest rate of 21.25%, it is quite possible that you will end up paying twice that amount ($5,400) before you fully pay off your college debt. If you paid $150 a month, it would take two years for you to completely pay back the debt. And this amount does not include your student loan, rent, or car payments; not to mention your daily living expenses. Collecting credit cards and credit card debt is detrimental to your financial future. It is equivalent to being on academic probation. You will have to work really hard and make some very key changes in order to get back on your feet. Do you really want to be on financial probation as soon as you get out of college?

Prevention:

Preventing financial probation right out of college is easier than you think. All you have to do is monitor the amount of debt you accrue while in school. The less debt you have, the better off you will be. While in school, if you

Honestly, credit cards are not baseball cards and should not be collected.

do not have the money to pay for something beforehand, do not charge it on your credit card. Credit cards should be used for convenience, not as a short-term loan. If you do not have the money to pay for what you charge or you will not realistically have the money before the bill is due, you should not charge it.

I understand the reality that most college students have credit cards and thus it is hard to advocate no credit cards. But I feel that it is only necessary to have 1-2 credit cards while you are in school. The limits should be low enough to handle on any given month. If you only make $500 a month while in school, it is not wise to have a credit card with a $5,000 credit limit. Budgeting experts recommend that your credit limit be no more than twice what you make monthly.

Also, research the credit card offers before signing up for them. You must remember that credit card companies are out to make large profits from uneducated consumers. I know it hurts your eyes but read the fine print. Go online and look for reviews of the credit card offer that you receive in the mail. See what other people say about the credit card that you are about to get. You may find that they have hidden fees, their interest rates change without notice, or the offer that they use to hook you in may not be as generous as it seems.

Here is an example that hits close to home:

I know you have seen them at your school; I'm talking about the credit card company employees that camp out at the most popular places on campus. They offer you a cool new credit card, plus a gift. All they need is

Credit card companies don't want to be your friend, and they don't want to help you!

your college ID. They don't run a credit check and they don't charge you a fee for opening a credit card account with them.

They tell you that they want to be the first company to give you an opportunity to build your credit and they want to prove it to you by offering you your own credit card. Credit Card companies don't want to be your friend and they don't want to help you!

What they really want to be is the first company that puts you into debt. They want to be the first to collect money in interest charges. Did you know that 74% of adults have the same credit card they had in college? It's true. This is truly music to the credit card company's ears. If they can get you to sign up as a freshman, they have a good chance of collecting money from you for decades. In order to do that, they will tell you anything under the sun to get you to sign up for their credit card.

They will make the process easy (college ID only), they will hook you in (no annual fees), and sweeten the deal (free gift). You should never sign up for a credit card with a bank that tries to coerce you with a cool gift.

A gift is nothing more than misdirection. They want you to focus on the gift and not the astronomical interest rate they are charging you. Look past the gift and ask them about the terms of their credit card. Make sure to ask them about their interest rates, how often they are compounded, and how they fare against the competition. If they cannot give you a satisfactory answer to any of these questions, it is time to walk away.

I understand that credit card terms and conditions can be confusing and I am here to help. You should never feel like you have to make financial commitments on your own. I recommend that you talk to an expert before you decide. You can talk to a parent, a close relative, or even a friend.

> *If you have questions about a credit card offer, feel welcome to visit www.copoket.co*

I would like to suggest an alternative to generating a large amount of credit card debt while in school. Start with a secured credit card. Secured credit cards are cards with limits that are determined by the amount of money in your savings account. For example, if you have $500 in your secured savings account, you will have a credit limit of $500. Once you have established a secure relationship with the bank, you can request an unsecured credit card. As a result, you will have a lower interest rate than if you were to apply for a credit card with an unknown bank that is running a promotion. I will show an example of how to do this in chapter 12.

If you do not like the concept of a secured credit card, it would also be a good idea to ask your parents if they would be willing to have their name on your credit card account as well. This way, if there ever is an emergency where you cannot pay your bill, they will be able to help you out with the payment for that month. Even though the scope of this book teaches you how to build your credit and handle emergencies on your own, it is always an added bonus if you have a third party that can help if a real emergency arises.

Just make sure that you only ask for help from your third party after you have exhausted every effort on your own. Using someone else as a crutch will only lead to a dependency on others during emergencies and will slow your journey to financial independence. I do not want this to happen to you, so I have included a number of ways to handle emergencies on your own in chapter 7.

It should be noted that as a result of the change to the Fair Isaac credit reporting formula in March of 2008, being included on your parents' credit cards no longer helps your personal credit rating. This practice was thoroughly abused and is now no longer an option for college students to begin building their credit.

For now, let's move on to other college mistakes.

2. Not Living Within Your Means

This is the second most common mistake made by college students. In a capitalist society, all lifestyles aren't created equal. Some families are better off than others. Some college students have a large amount of discretionary income backed by their parents while others are paying tuition on their own. Every college student has a different financial reality. Many students make the mistake of trying to keep up with trendsetters at their school and getting themselves into financial trouble.

Make sure to live within your means and not fall victim to unsafe spending habits. If you can stay within your budget in college, you will be rewarded greatly after you graduate. I don't want budgeting to sound like a bore or a burden because it isn't. I am not suggesting that you never go shopping; I love to shop as well. I only suggest that you make sure that you understand what discretionary money is. It is not your entire monthly salary. Instead, it is the money that you have left over after budgeting for your recurring expenses. Taking care of these expenses is most important.

It is also vital to keep your recurring expenses (including food) separate from your budget for shopping for material and luxury items. This way, if you spend all of your discretionary money, you do not have to worry about whether or not you will be able to pay your bills for the month. This can be achieved by having different checking accounts or any other method that keeps the two spending categories separate.

An important tip to note is that you can only shop with the money from your discretionary fund. If you are at a point where you cannot afford all of the items that you have in your cart, put an item or two back until you can afford it. At this point in your life, no material item is so necessary that it is worth risking your financial future in order to get it.

3. Keeping track of Credit Card Debt

Most students adopt the "Out of Sight Out of Mind" philosophy when it comes to debt. This is the wrong attitude to have. Even though you may have forgotten about your debt, the people or companies that you owe haven't forgotten about you! Here is an example to prove our point:

Remember the time you loaned your friend some money and they didn't pay you back? Is it not true that every time you saw them afterward, the thought of them owing you money crossed your mind? I thought so!

Keeping track of your current debt is important because the longer you wait to pay back your debt, the more you will end up paying in the long run. Most students lose track of their current debt when they are indebted to too many creditors.

> *Make sure that you total the amount of your monthly bills so that you know how much money you will have once your bills have been paid.*

If you ever do find yourself owing money to multiple people or companies, create a central place in which you have every expenditure for that month in front of you so that you don't accidentally forget to pay a bill. For example, if you just received your credit card statement, put the statement with the rest of the bills for the month so that you can pay them all at once.

Even better, most banks have online bill payment systems. When you receive the bill, put the amount and date due in your online bill payment system and you won't have to worry about it. My only caution is to make sure that you total the amount of your monthly bills so that you know how much money you will have once your bills have been paid. I do not want you to either not have enough to pay your bills or overdraw your account because your bills are more of your budget than expected.

4. Not Saving For Emergencies

Not saving for emergencies is like going SCUBA diving without an oxygen tank; it is possible to survive but highly unlikely. An emergency fund is your first line of defense if anything ever goes wrong. Most times you will find yourself in a situation where you will need quick cash and will not have a fast way to get it. When this happens, you can tap into your emergency fund to help you overcome your financial emergency.

There used to be a time when you didn't have to worry about an emergency fund because one was always two doors down. That emergency fund was your parents. For some, their parents are still their emergency fund. While in college, you will find that your newfound independence will lead to at least one emergency situation. While on your own in college, start an emergency fund. On average, most people allocate about 5-10% of their income after taxes to emergencies.

This way, if there is ever the need for an emergency trip home, unexpected parking fine, or another textbook you didn't know you needed, the emergency fund will be the resource that you would tap into. This method beats out applying for a small loan and having to pay interest on it. I go into further detail on emergency funds in chapter 7.

5. Misallocating Student Loan Money

Every dollar that you borrow today must be paid back with interest at some point in your life. Knowing that, it would be wise to only ask for as much money as you need while you are in college. This does not mean that you must only take out enough money for tuition; many people ask for enough to pay for their full tuition, room and board, plus books. It is also not uncommon for individuals to take out an extra $1,000-$1,500 to pay for their food expenses and other necessities so that they do not have to worry about working for food while they are in school. These are all very noteworthy ways to use student loan money.

On the other hand, many people feel like student loan dollars is free money that can be spent on anything. I have heard of individuals using their student loan money to start a business, while others have borrowed extra money to lease extravagant homes near their school. One person went as far as to borrow an additional $12,000 to purchase a brand new motorcycle that he crashed the first day he got it! These are all unacceptable reasons to borrow money intended for tuition or room and board.

If you are someone who has used student loan money for miscellaneous reasons, don't worry—it is not the end of the world. What I would advise is take some extra money annually and start paying down the principal on your loan. This way, by the time you graduate, you would have paid off the extra amount that you borrowed without having to pay any interest on it.

6. Going to the Wrong Places for Emergency Cash

It is going to happen at one point in your life. You are going to be pressed for cash and you will not have a friend or relative who you can contact to get the funds. More students have this problem than you think! The worst thing to do when you are in this situation is to try a cash advance or payday loan company. It is very easy to spot these scam artists.

Here are a few tip-offs that you may be dealing with a payday loan or cash advance facility:

Does the sign on top of the store happen to say "Payday Loans"?!?!?	If so, chances are you are dealing with a payday loan facility.
Do they advertise that they will give you a loan with little to no credit?	If they do, it is very likely that they are running a cash advance company.
Are there any advertisements that promote "Your job is your credit"?	If they do, that is a sure-fire tip off that they are a pay day loan facility.

Bonus: If any employee in the building is not wearing at least a collared shirt, I would advise you to just turn right around and get back in your car!

Payday loan and cash advance companies are bad news. They charge astronomical interest rates on a very small loan and usually make about two to four times the principal amount on the original loan. Never take out a loan from these places and tell everyone that you know that they are a really bad idea.

7. *Forgetting about Scholarships & Grants*

I have been talking to college students for quite a while on the issue of money and I have noticed that almost every student overlooks this point. There are literally thousands of scholarships and grants out there for students who are already enrolled in college. Most students just don't apply for them because they feel that an extra essay or two is more work than they can handle. Instead, they just take out more loans.

The problem with this logic is that they will have to do almost 11 times as much work when they get into the workforce to pay off the principal and interest on that additional loan than if they were to write the original essay for the scholarship. This is the closest to free money that most college students will see for a very long time.

What's more important is that most college students adopt the "it's too much work" philosophy and don't apply. This is very good news for you because it means that there is less competition. Think of it this way. Scholarships that you earn while in college are equivalent to being paid for being a good student. Every dollar that you receive today will save you at least $1.25 in the future when you count compounding interest. This could very well mean that it will take you 22 years to pay off a 30-year loan. Or better yet, it will take you about seven years to pay off a 10-year loan when you earn that additional scholarship while in college.

8. Calculating Automobile Costs Incorrectly

This was one of the problems that I had when I first got my car. I assumed that when I bought the car, all I would have to do is pay the monthly payments and spend about $60 a month on gas. Easy enough right? Wrong!

Not only did I have to spend more than $100 a month on gas, but I forgot about insurance! Not only did I forget insurance, but I forgot about oil changes, tune-ups, car washes, vacuuming, and parking fees. All of these could cost an additional $750-$3000 dollars a year—and that is not counting insurance.

Before you think about bringing your car with you to school, consider how much it is going to cost to keep it there. Track the average cost to fill up your tank on a weekly basis. See if your university offers free parking or whether you have to pay a monthly or even a daily fee!

All these things must be taken into consideration before they become a real burden and you have to tap into that emergency fund for something like a routine oil change.

9. Not Seeking Out Competitive Bank Rates

Choosing the correct bank takes research and a lot of patience. One of the most common mistakes that individuals make is choosing a bank using the newspaper, television ads, or from their parents. I am honestly not advocating that you don't listen your parents; I am only suggesting that you use them as a basis for your own research. Make sure to look for banks that have lower interest rates and are hungry for new business. Don't go with the first student loan offer that comes in the mail. Also, don't rush to consolidate your student loan debt without going to a college financial aid counselor or talking to your parents.

Then it is time for you to get a checking and savings account, make sure to look for a bank that does not charge many fees. Fees can add up and I don't want you ending up paying more than you have to. Also, look for a

There are a number of online banks that offer annual savings yields above 5% - you can find a few at www.copocket.co

higher-yielding savings account. If the bank at your school only offers 2%, but the bank five miles away offers 4%, it would be wise to go with the bank five miles away.

I understand that convenience is the key when you are in college. But isn't more money in your bank account more convenient than traveling a few miles? If you agree, go ahead and get the higher-yield savings account. There are a number of online banks that offer annual 5%. If you are serious about your financial future, it would be wise to look into a high-yield savings account while in school.

10. Not shopping for the best prices on everyday items

University stores and your school's bookstore are not always the best place to pick up your everyday items. If you are at a school where these two places are your only option, you might be limited in the selections available to you. But if you are at a school that has a grocery store or a small shop in a residential neighborhood, traveling to buy your toothpaste and deodorant will probably be your best bet. Taking that trip to an alternate place can save you up to $100 a semester as university facilities are usually overpriced.

Conclusion

Safeguarding yourself against these top 10 college mistakes can save you thousands of dollars a semester. More importantly, it will help you develop the very habits that will help you become financial free in life.

Now that we have discussed these pitfalls, it is up to you to avoid them. Let's take some time now to look at how you will make your money in college. If there is anything that you feel that I may have missed, go to www.copocket.co and check out my more detailed list.

Review

1. Credit cards should be used for convenience, not as a short term loan.

2. If you remain patient about your finances, learn to live within your means, and save up for emergencies, handling your finances in college will be a breeze.

3. Just because your debt is out of your mind doesn't mean it is out of the mind of the people you owe.

4. Payday Loan stores and cash advance facilities are not adequate places to get emergency money.

5. Student loans should be used for school. Never borrow more than you absolutely need!

6. Don't forget about scholarships and grants!

7. Make sure to shop around for competitive rates.

Review Questions

1. How do you know when you are getting the best rate on a credit card?

2. What should you do when you are strapped for cash and have no one to borrow from?

3. What is the maximum amount of money you should borrow from a payday loan facility? (Hint: It's the only number that can't be positive or negative)

Chapter 3

Identifying Your True College Income

"I'm living so far beyond my income that we may almost be said to be living apart." -E.E Cummings

In this chapter I'll talk about how to determine your true income while in school. Identifying where your money will come from in college is a very important step toward effective budgeting. Students, though, rarely take the time to figure this out so they never know how much money they truly have to budget every month. Before you start budgeting, you must know exactly how much you have saved and how much additional money will come to you in the future. This way, you will be better equipped to calculate how much you can spend on recurring expenses and how much additional money you may need to come up with to afford your time at school.

There are a number of ways a college student can earn income. Whenever my older brother needed some quick cash while in college, he would run straight to the blood bank and make a donation. If he was going out on a date, he would make a trip to the sperm bank as well. Don't ask me why, he just did it. I knew that I never wanted to be like that; so I decided that I was going to learn how to budget the money that I already had so that I didn't have to take a monthly trip to the blood bank.

This chapter will go over four different revenue streams in detail and easy ways to maximize your income while still allowing you to have most of the things that you want. The four income streams are employment, student loans, college savings, and any money that you may be able to borrow. Each of these income streams are important and can take you a long way in college. Learning how to manage all four at once will help you bolster your budgeting skills while still having fun in school.

Employment

According to the 2013 annual report published by Jump$tart.org, 84% of college students hold paid summer jobs, but only 51% use any of their money to help with expenses.. This means that one third of college students spend all their summer money before they even get to school. This is a real shame because any summer money can really go a long way while they are in school.

More than 70% of college students have a job at some point while they are in school. Most university jobs are easy enough. I know most of the jobs that I had required sitting at a desk and painstakingly finishing my homework assignments. It honestly was torture getting paid to do my homework.

Imagine yourself at school, sitting at a comfortable desk with your homework in front of you, and you are getting paid to do it! That doesn't sound like a bad job does it? It is essentially an in-school scholarship. In-school scholarships are university jobs that pay you to do next to nothing; as a result, you use that time to do your homework.

A good place to look for in-school scholarships is the employment bulletin board at your school or your school's employment website.

You want to take advantage of every in-school scholarship that you can because they are beneficial income streams that are relatively easy to obtain.

Let's break down what some in-school scholarship examples could be for you. Is there a job at your school that allows students to monitor who enters your school's dormitories? These are usually low-intensity jobs with a lot of down time that allows you to do your homework on a regular basis. This is an awesome job to have because most of the time you will have a quiet place to study with very little distractions.

Second, is there a job at your school that allows you to sit on the phone for hours trying to get alumni contributions? Most students shy away from this job because they either don't like talking to unknown people or they think that they will spend too much time on the phone and will not be able to get their homework done. It has been my experience, and the reported experience of students at a couple dozen other schools, that most of the time you are just sitting there listening to the phone ring. You would be lucky if you reach 10 people an hour. And if you reach those people, most will not be interested and let you know within the first couple seconds of the conversation.

So, on average, you will possibly only talk to six people per hour for more than two minutes. Including the dialing and the phone number research (if your system is not automated); you should spend no more than 25 minutes an hour doing actual work. This means that you are studying for 35 minutes an hour on someone else's dollar. Not bad for a college student. Those kinds of jobs are usually reserved for high-ranking government officials.

Third, most work study jobs are very low intensity. If you work in an academic department with a subject matter that requires a lot of reading (philosophy and English), there is a strong chance that the bulk of your job will be copying papers, which can be done without any real effort from you.

These departments usually give out a lot of papers, which professors don't allow students to grade, so you won't be stuck grading a professor's multiple choice midterm exam. On average, you spend about 15 minutes an hour doing actual work. The rest of the time you will be able to find a desk and get some reading done before your next class. Or better yet, you can finish that paper that you neglected to do because your favorite show's season finale was on!

Getting the Right Job: Finding the on-campus jobs is the easy part. The hard part is narrowing down which job will pay you the most money WHILE allowing you to do the least amount of work. One job might pay you more but you are working 40 minutes out of the hour. This is not the job that you want if you are looking to get paid to study. On the other hand, another job may pay you a dollar or two less but you work half as much. I advise you to get this job.

Once you figure out which job you are going to take, sit down and calculate exactly how much you will earn every two weeks. This is, in fact, the reason you applied for the job in the first place. You need to determine exactly how much you are going to earn every two weeks. This way, you know exactly how much you will have for recurring expenses every month.

You can also take care of your variable expenses with your college wages. Keep in mind your college wages might not be enough to cover your variable expenses and you may have to tap into your reserves from time to time. Your college wages should be used primarily for your recurring expenses. The money you make from your job in school should allow you to pay for items like your phone bill. But if your recurring expenses are not enough, you may have to tap into other sources. Let's take some time to talk about student loans.

Student Loans

If you talk to ten different people about what to do with student loan money, you will likely get ten different answers. Some will tell you that you should spend it on books, others on superfluous things. Others will tell you that you should save it for a rainy day and still others will tell you to blow it on something really nice for yourself. Do you want to know the right answer to this question? The answer might surprise you.

Every one of the above answers is correct. Your student loan money should be used for whatever you NEED. And it is always healthy to take a little bit of your extra student loan money (no more than 10% of what's left) to buy something nice for yourself: you deserve it!

In all seriousness, there are things that you should not spend your student loan money on. It is not wise to take out loan money to purchase a new car, go on a shopping spree, or buy a house. If there is that much extra money from your loans, it is quite possible that you took out too much and will have to pay more money when you get out of college. It honestly is not worth it!

If you do have extra money from your student loans, it would be very wise to start paying down the principal amount. If you do not wish to just yet, you can take the extra money and put it in a savings or money market account for emergencies. Your student loan money can also be used to pay for books, supplies, or necessities that you may need for school. It SHOULD NOT be used to buy frivolous goods; you will end up paying for that mistake at a time when you need money most: when you are out on your own after college!

Savings

Most forget about the amount of extra dollars needed to pay for supplemental college education costs. There are lab fees, tickets home, vacations, and textbooks. For that reason, many people have college savings plans set up before they even get to college. These savings plans, if used correctly, can go a long way toward financial stability and much needed college brain food (Pizza!).

The typical college-bound student enters college with about $12,000 saved for tuition, books, room and board. This amount, although large, won't pay for one year's tuition at most universities. Today, most universities will add that amount to your estimated family contribution and it will leave your family's account before you get a chance to spend it! Your college savings should be used for your tuition, and anything left over should be used for your books for that semester. If you have anything left over after those two expenditures, save the additional money for your books the following semester.

A lot of students make the mistake of spending the extra money that they have saved without considering they must pay for books the next semester. Then, they have to take money already allocated for other things or take out additional loans to pay for their second semester of books. I do not want this to happen to you. So instead of thinking that you have an extra $450 to do what you please, place that money back into your savings account and wait for your second round of book shopping to come around.

Ok, in all seriousness, I know that you are not going to place the entire $450 back into your savings account. I was a college student once and fully understand how cash sometimes just magically converts itself into food, basketball tickets, and shoes. Although saving it is what you should ideally do, try to at least keep about $300 in savings. That way, you won't have to find as much money when you have to buy books next semester.

Borrowing

Finally, the last form of income that I will go over with you will be borrowing. Some students never have the liberty of borrowing from friends or family while others do. If you have the privilege of borrowing money from a relative, make sure you have a solid plan to pay them back.

Work on a timetable for repayment; even if it doesn't begin until after you graduate. Let them know exactly what you are borrowing the money for and don't be afraid to add an extra incentive by telling them that you will give the money back with a little interest. Most won't accept interest but it is still nice to offer. You can then take the loan and use it for whatever you need. You can use that money for tuition, emergencies, books, or just to have some cash flow in the budget every month.

Conclusion

It is very important to tie all of your income streams together while you are in college. Take your student wages and use them to pay off your recurring expenses while using your student loan money to pay for your yearly expenses. Use your borrowings to pay for variable expenses while saving a large chunk of it for emergencies and investments. I go into greater detail about what to do with extra cash in chapter 6, but it is important to note here that extra money should not be misallocated.

If you don't take anything else from this book, please remember this: extra money properly allocated today can and will lead to a lot more money in your pocket tomorrow. And every saved dollar properly put away today will lead you well on your way to financial success in college and in life!

Review

1. It is important to know exactly how much money you will have throughout the year so that you can determine how much you will have for recurring expenses.

2. Make sure to capitalize on in-school scholarships.

3. Don't borrow more student loan money than you have to.

4. Get an adequate picture of how much money you have monthly, per semester, and annually and it help you stay financially healthy in college.

Review Questions

1. What are the four types of college income and how should each be used?

2. What are three in-school scholarships at your school?

3. What should you do if you have some extra student loan money?

4. Of the four types of income discussed, which should be used for recurring expenses?

5. What is the craziest thing you have either bought or heard that someone bought with student loan money?

Chapter 4

Determining Budget Categories

"If your outgo exceeds your income, then your upkeep is your downfall." -Anonymous

The biggest mistake that college students make when it comes to budgeting is fitting their spending into someone else's categories. Hundreds of thousands of college students spend a significant portion of their money on material possessions. Usually, they jump onto the latest trends or try to keep up with friends. As a result, they find themselves in really bad financial positions. A few mistakes made in college will be a huge financial burden all the way into your 30s. This is not a position that I want you to be in.

What do I mean by living in someone else's spending category? It means you pick up their spending habits and do not live within the limits that you have set for yourself; if you have set them at all. An example of this is going shopping with your friends and spending money that was allocated for something else. Another example is going out with your friends and spending your entire budgeted grocery amount on one or two meals. A third example is putting an item on your credit card that you do not have the money to pay because a friend has it, or you think that it would be cool to have one.

These are excellent examples of what it means to live in someone else's spending category. You must realize that most of the people around you do not have a sound financial plan. They are either spending their parent's money, which gets rejuvenated every time the kid throws a fit or after they have recklessly spent their parent's hard-earned money on temporary material possessions.

This is Not Who You Are.

There is a time and place to spend money on material possessions. It is imperative to remember to budget the amount that you are going to spend before you leave the house with that cash or credit/debit card. By doing it the opposite way you will consistently find yourself overspending your budget.

Living within your means is just as important as getting an "A" on any final exam. Many students have a rather false idealistic fantasy that they will not have to manage their finances because a high-paying job right out of college will yield them the opportunity to make enough money where they won't have to worry about how much they spend. If I may, let me give a brief newsflash.

The most successful people all know how to manage their own budget. There is not one truly wealthy person that does not take an active role in managing their finances. They budget constantly and know where and how their money is being spent. Because they are aware, they have all their necessities taken care of and they have the freedom to buy the finer things in life. But they do not make this conscious choice until they know that they have all their essential budgeting categories taken care of.

Most people new to the world of financial management do the exact opposite and get themselves into trouble. They are in such a rush to live like the rich and famous that they fail to see how living lavishly now will result in their depleted wealth in the future.

I want you to do me a favor. Raise your right hand and promise yourself something. I want you to stand up right now, with your hand in the air, and say:

"I promise to live within my means no matter what."

It seems silly, but it truly does work. If you can stick to living within your means for the formative years of your financial education, I can guarantee you that you will be able to accomplish your financial dreams. With that said, it is time to figure out what your financial categories are and how you can use them to live within your means.

What is Important to You?

Everyone's financial categories are different. They are different because everyone spends money on different things and we all need to allocate different amounts to the lifestyle that we want to live. As a college student, your lifestyle should be geared toward creating a better life for yourself out of college. This does not mean that you cannot buy things for yourself nor have tons of fun. It just means that you should take the time to learn about budgeting and how to do it efficiently while you are in school so it is one less thing to learn when you graduate. Believe me, you want to learn how to budget before your home, food, and livelihood depends on it.

You are the best person to determine what your budget categories should be. You will need to narrow down your absolutely necessary expenditures and be as detailed as possible

For help determining your budget categories, go to www.copocket.co and look under free tools.

about how much you will have to spend in each one of the

categories. For example, do you live in a dormitory or an apartment off campus? If you live in a dormitory, you do not have to worry about creating a budget category for rent and utilities. Instead, you can take that money and allocate it for another category.

The basic budget categories have been described in detail in previous chapters. It is very important to know what your recurring and variable expenses are so that you will efficaciously be able to budget them. Realistically, the less that you have to budget for at this stage in your budgeting education, the better off you will be in the long run when you are managing millions. Let's take a look at some of the categories that you may exclude now but will more than likely have to include in the future.

Do you have a meal plan at your school? If you do, you do not need to allocate as much money to your food budget. It is my advice that you keep a food budget category because we all know how easy it is to get sick of cafeteria food. When this happens, you can take the money from your food budget and buy groceries or go out to eat—just no more than once or twice a week. A change of scenery and food selection is always healthy—unless the nickname of your new choice of food is "Heart Attack on a Bun!"

Aside from the obvious categories of expenses that have been mentioned in previous chapters, it is vital that you budget items like clothes, food, and fun activities in as much detail as you can. This way, when it is time to spend money on these items, you already have a set goal amount that you are willing to spend and anything over that amount you know will take away from another necessity. The goal here is fiscal responsibility and that comes with a detailed plan.

Conclusion

At this point, I have gone over the basics of what needs to be budgeted and why it is important for everything to be budgeted. I hope I was able to set the framework for the rest of the book. And as you continue, I want you to keep thinking about the basic concepts that have been included here when you are going over advanced budgeting, building your credit, and reaching for financial freedom by 30.

I would advise you to read over these chapters as many times as you need until you have internalized the concepts and the importance of having an organized budget plan. This will help you greatly throughout your entire life; not just in school. Next, I am going to look at some advanced budgeting techniques and how to have your new budgeting skills work toward your success in the real world.

Review

1. Make sure to live within your means and not someone else's.

2. Only you can determine your budget categories because only you know how you want to live.

3. Remember to take care of your recurring expenses first.

4. Taking 15 minutes to create a detailed budget category diagram will greatly help you determine where your income will be allocated.

5. Don't be afraid to eat something besides cafeteria food.

Review Questions

1. Have you gone to http://copocket.co/to check out the additional resources available, yet?

2. Where do you see yourself at 30?

3. What are your three most important financial goals for this year?

4. What are three things you can do to achieve them?

Chapter 5

What Are Your Financial Goals?

"The secret of all victory lies in the organization of the non-obvious."
-Marcus Aurelius

At the very beginning of my journey as a Financial Antermologist I was very optimistic. When I first started studying, I immediately thought that I was going to have thousands of dollars saved up in my first six months! The truth is, I didn't even end up *earning* a thousand dollars in my first six months. It was discouraging. I thought maybe all of this wasn't for me. In despair, I put a call in to my mentor to let him know how I felt.

When I told him how I was feeling, I got the exact opposite answer I was expecting. I thought he was going to agree that this program might not be the best thing for me at the time. Instead, in a rather forceful tone I might add, he told me that this is the exact time that I should start budgeting my money. I have paraphrased the speech that he gave me below:

"So let me get this straight, you believe millionaires begin to learn how to budget the second they make their first million? Of course they don't; they mastered budgeting years before the money rolled in. Most that have picked themselves up by their bootstraps have had it very hard at first. And the only thing that saved them was their grasp on financial concepts.

Even though everything else may not have been working,

they were still able to afford the bare necessities that kept their life and their business afloat. The same tools that they used to help them survive are now helping them flourish after things have started going right. And for that reason, they will never be broke again a day in their lives.

Right now, you are surviving. You are learning to budget and save a little so that it will not be that hard when you have a lot. Having a large amount of money is more responsibility than you think, and if you are not careful, you could put yourself in more trouble than when you didn't have money. Learning to budget will greatly reduce the likelihood that you will find yourself in a real financial bind. For you to tell me that you don't think that proper budgeting at any point in your life is for you shows me that you are completely missing the point. Here, let me give you a scenario of what could happen when you don't know how to budget.

Think about the number of lottery winners that have won more money than one person can spend in a lifetime. And guess what, they are now as broke as you are and have gone back to the same situation that made them resort to purchasing lottery tickets in the first place. They either lost it all from spending too much money on houses, furniture, and cars without considering how much they have spent or they neglected to think about the tax obligations that millionaires must satisfy. Many chose bad accountants that took advantage of their success: anything!

You must learn to budget so that you are in control of your money at all times.

Listen, I know you have what it takes to learn how to budget your money. I have talked to you about the importance of having your finances in order and saving up for emergencies. This is the one task in your life that you should not expect *someone to handle for you. Doing so will put you in a position where you will have to trust that someone else has your best interest at heart. And if they're running a business, do you think they have your best interest in mind or making money.*

Now that's actually a trick question. Because some will try to keep your best interest at heart, but most will not! And why would you want to take that gamble with something as important as your financial future? I know I wouldn't. I don't want you to, either. I want you to learn how to budget pennies now so millions will not be hard later. I know you have what it takes; it's time for you to believe in yourself."

That speech put a lot of things into perspective for me. I realized that this process was going to be slow at first and that it hopefully was going to pick up weeks, months, or maybe even years down the line. But I knew when it did pick up, I was going to be ready! I had to be ready because if I wasn't, I was going to find myself in a situation where I had all this extra money but no real way to make it work in my favor. This defeated the entire purpose of budgeting my money properly.

I hope that speech inspired you as well. It really outlined the importance of budgeting and the importance of having just a little bit of patience in the very beginning.

I want to take this time right now to help you set up your financial goals. These goals are going to be the driving force behind why you budget. They are important because if you do not have a goal with anything that you do, you will find it hard to motivate yourself to do an efficient job. Now, let's narrow down what motivates you to bolster your budgeting skills.

Why Are You Budgeting?

Take out a sheet of paper and a pen.

On that sheet of paper, I want you to make two columns. Label the first column: "Why I shouldn't budget" and the other column: "My Ultimate Wish List." Fill out the "Why I shouldn't budget" side first by writing down every reason that you have against budgeting this very second. It could be personal, financial, spiritual, or even comical! Spend as much time as you need writing down every reason you can think of.

Done? Great! Now on the other half of your paper, I want you to have a little fun. Write in the "My Ultimate Wish List" column everything that you ever want to have in your lifetime that you can't afford right now. It can be anything from a new video game system to a multi- level super-mansion off the coast of Madagascar. It can be whatever you want out of life. I had one person make this ultimate wish list:

· A submarine

· A ticket to outer space

· My own private island

· A Chimp named Mr. Jumparound

· A Liger (A lion-tiger hybrid)

· A signed copy of one of Carmen Electra's breast implants

· A 50 room mansion

· Ooooh, and a hybrid car!

I'm honestly not making that list up! He was really excited to show it to me. I use his list to help you see that you are free to be as elaborate as you want; it is your list. Take as much time as you need and be sure to have as much fun as you can when creating your list.

> *You will not learn anything from doing nothing at all.*

Finished? Excellent! The purpose of constructing the list was so that you can compare and contrast your reasons for wanting to budget efficiently and your reasons for not budgeting. Now go back and revisit the first list that you made on reasons you shouldn't budget.

As you look over that list, are there any adequate reasons to not start working toward getting everything that you want on your ultimate wish list? Are these financial issues or laziness issues? Are you too busy to start right now? Do you think that it is too complicated? Do you feel that it won't work? Do you honestly lack the willpower? These are all good reasons to not begin to develop the discipline to budget properly?

But they are not good enough reasons to not achieve everything that you want out of life!

Great things come from commitment. They come from stepping out of your comfort zone and taking risks. Sometimes the risks do not pay off, oftentimes they do. The important thing is that no matter if the risks pay off or not, you still learn a valuable life lesson; remember you learn from your mistakes as well as your successes. You don't learn anything from doing nothing at all!

If you need to start small, start small. Start by determining your budget categories. Figure out what you spend money on every month and how much you spend on average. This will give you a more accurate view of your finances and will get you more comfortable with understanding how you need to set up your budgeting plan. When you are ready, start calculating your recurring expenses and start brainstorming how you pay for your recurring expenses every month. After you do this, start calculating how much money you have on average every month after your recurring expenses are taken care of. Then, move on to other expenses like variable or yearly expenses.

If you take a trip once a year, try to figure out a way that you can manipulate your budget so that you don't have to come up with the money all at once. Put yourself on a savings plan. Start putting 5%-10% of the money that you earn into a savings account. It's not about the value; it's about the action. I want you to get comfortable with managing your money and knowing its whereabouts. Once you do that, creating a master budget will be a lot easier.

If you are up to it and want to start creating a master budget, let's move on. If you are not at that point yet, don't worry. Read the information in this section anyhow to become familiar with the concepts. It will help you become more comfortable with budgeting.

Managing Your Finances

At this point, you should have already established what all of your expenses are. You have created your budget categories, and you have made a commitment to creating a master budget. Now all you have to do is start budgeting. This means making sure you know where your money is going every month and where that money will come from.

You should have a "bills only" checking account that is used solely for recurring expenses. This way you won't have to worry about spending too much money and not having enough to cover your bare necessities.

Since you have a pretty accurate picture of how much money you will spend on your recurring expenses every month, you should put that amount into your "bills only" checking account. It would be great to find a bank that allows online bill paying. Some of the banks nowadays have sophisticated systems where they will withdraw the money automatically and pay the bill on the designated day that you choose. This way you do not have to worry about making late payments. That is perfect for you because a late payment or two on your credit report right now will mean that you have to work exponentially harder to recover. We'll dig deeper into credit in part two of this book.

You can have another account that will be used for your variable expenses. This doesn't have to be another checking account, although it can be. You just have to make sure that you have a safe place to store the money for when you need it.

I'm not saying that you must go out and get a separate account for each individual budget category; I am only suggesting that you get a separate account for paying your bills. If you want to keep your variable and

> *Remember, if you bury money or if you have it sitting in a damp place hiding it from yourself too long, it will mold.*

annual expenses in the same account, that is fine, just make sure that you have it written down somewhere how much of the money is allocated to what. I prefer that you also have these funds in a savings or money market account. This way you can earn interest on the money while you are saving it. Taking these steps should give you an organized list of your expenses, how you will pay for it, and where the money will come from. With all of your finances in order, you can spend more time worrying about other things like studying. Or better yet, you can spend more time figuring out what awesome place you would like to visit for spring break! On top of that, you now have a plan to start saving for it.

Make Sure to Stay on Top of Your Finances

The most important part of budgeting is knowing when to adjust your plan. When doing your budget, new situations may arise daily that will warrant adjusting your money allocation priorities. It is your job to determine what is important enough to adjust your plans and what isn't. Most of the time, the new cause will not warrant you making an adjustment, but sometimes it does. And when it does, you must thoroughly work through your budget to make sure it works best for you.

Let me give you an example from my life. For most of my sophomore year in college, I didn't have a cell phone. It was not that I couldn't afford one; I just no longer wanted to deal with it ringing off of the hook all the time. In the summer of my sophomore, I started a new company.

This company required me to be in the field often. As a result, I was missing a large amount of phone calls. My business partner advised (demanded!) that I get a cell phone. We ended up picking out a high-tech phone with all the latest bells and whistles designed for the mobile businessman. Everyone was convinced that this phone was a must have.

The question of cost then came up. Will I be able to afford another recurring expense? I had invested a lot of money into the start of my new company and there was no guarantee that it would be profitable anytime soon. I could have to spend more money on surprise expenses. What would happen if I had to invest a lot more and could no longer afford the cost of this new expense?

I crunched the numbers and realized that I shouldn't add an extra $140 a month to my recurring expenses. At that point, I had to make a choice. I chose to not add the recurring expense. If I did, my monthly recurring expenses (minus rent) would have been more than $800 a month. That was more than I was comfortable with paying on a monthly basis. So instead, I chose a cheaper phone with a cheaper plan and everything turned out fine. That is a direct example from my life.

Still, there are too many scenarios to name in this book that will merit adjusting your budgeting plan; that would take up an entire book within itself. Honestly, I'm not the person to determine what merits you adjusting your budget anyhow. If you do decide that you must adjust your budget, make sure to take a step back and look at the entire picture. Adding new things to your budget has a ripple effect on your entire plan, so make sure you plan for the added adjustments. Let's run through a few basic things that you should think about when adjusting your budget.

Are you adding another recurring expense? If you are, you need to figure out how you are going to pay for it. Are you going to take money from variable expenses? Are you going to work more hours? Will you get a new job? No matter what the case, make sure you know how you are going to afford the recurring expense before adding it to the budget.

Do you have a surprise expense? Surprise expenses can be a real problem when you have an organized budget. And they are even a worse problem when you don't—I guarantee it! When your money is properly budgeted, you will be better equipped to know where you will get the money for what you need.

Do you have to tap into your emergency fund? Will you be able to pay for it by switching some expenses around?
Can you afford to buy in bulk for a little while to save money on grocery bills? Can you use some of the money that you saved for annual expenses and replace it later when the emergency is over? There are literally hundreds of different things that you can do, but you severely limit your options if you don't have an organized budget already in place.

Do you have extra money coming in? Extra money can mean several different things. It can either mean that you have more money to save or you have a little extra money to spend. If you choose to save some of it, which you should no matter what, I will show you how to use extra money to your advantage in the next chapter on advanced budgeting techniques.

It is not against the rules for you to take extra cash that you have and buy something nice for yourself. Just make sure you do not spend it all. Take 10% and put it in your savings account. Also, take at least 10% of it and put it in your emergency fund. I'm sure that 10% will help you out a lot more when you have an unexpected emergency than that shirt you just had to have from your favorite store.

Conclusion

There are countless scenarios that will come up when you are budgeting. The important thing is to make sure that you remain level headed about the decisions that you make. Adding more expenses to your budget only stretches your budget thin. If you can afford it, do it. If you can't, either devise a way to make more money or figure out a way to change some things in your budget so that you can.

Your plan should also have a finite time limit. The budget that you have for yourself will usually change every semester if you are in college. There may be small adjustments in between semesters, but there more than likely will be major changes once you move to the next grade level.

You may choose to cancel your meal plan; your residence may cost more…anything. Make sure that whatever changes you make in your life, you adjust your budget accordingly so you can afford them.

Review

1. Creating a master budget does not happen overnight. The process may take time at first, but do not give up.

2. Budgeting pennies today will make budgeting millions a lot easier tomorrow.

3. No reason for not budgeting will justify not having everything you want out of life.

4. Starting small is always better than not starting at all.

5. Once you start, keep at it. Staying on top of your finances has greater rewards than you can imagine.

6. Buying nice things for yourself is always nice; make sure you save a little bit of extra money as well, though.

Review Questions

1. What are the top three items on your ultimate wish list?

2. How much of your extra money should be allocated toward emergencies?

3. Who is the person best equipped to manage your finances?

Chapter 6

Advanced Budgeting

"Good management is better than good income."
-Portuguese Proverb

As you learn to budget like a Financial Antermologist, you will find that you have more extra money than you used to. This is a very nice feeling, believe me. However, we must not become slaves to those feelings. There are a number of people who get to this stage in the budgeting process and find it has become a liability instead of an asset. They make it a liability because they take the extra money and spend it on things that they should not have. This is no fault of their own; it is human nature to reward yourself for a job well done. I only want to suggest that it should be done in moderation.

It is not my place to tell you what to do with the extra money that you will accumulate when you follow a master budget. Instead, allow me to advise against certain activities:

- Do not take the money and add on an additional recurring expense unless you feel that it is absolutely necessary.

- Do not spend your entire saved amount on one item that will require more of your budgeted money in the future (ex. new cell phone, new car, and a new boa constrictor).

- Do not dip into your recurring expense account because the item that you want to purchase cannot be paid for with the extra money you have saved.

If you follow this advice, you should be in good shape.

Preparing to Manage Millions

But I would like to take budgeting one step further, if I may.

There is a way in which you can take the extra money that you save every month and make it work in your favor. With just a little effort on your part, the advanced budgeting techniques that I am about to introduce to you will almost surely put you on an expedited path to managing millions. If you want to know how to make thousands by saving a little extra cash, read on.

Still with me? Great! This program is simple. I have to give credit to T. Harv Ecker for this program. He is one of the most intelligent speakers on planning for your financial future I have ever had the privilege of hearing. All you have to do is take the extra cash that you have earned after effective budgeting and put it into a number of specialized budget categories. Each category will better your life in its own way and will make you a well-rounded person.

This plan requires that you create six new budget categories for your extra money. This does not mean that you have to open up a brand new savings account for each one; it just means that you must have a place to store the money in each category on its own so that you do not confuse what the funds are used for. The six categories are as follows:

- Long Term Savings- *10%*

- Money to Burn- *10%*

- Education- *10%*

- Philanthropy- *10%*

- Savings and Investments- *10%*

- Necessities- *50%*

Each one of these categories will receive different denominations of the extra cash you have each month after paying bills. This program is a fun way to encourage you to save more money, budget properly and work harder so that you can add more to these categories the next time around. Let's look at each one of these categories in detail.

Long-Term Savings: 10% of the extra money that you have should be allocated to long-term savings. The purpose of this account is to accumulate wealth. This means that you are not allowed to take money out of this account...ever. That's right; you are never allowed to spend this money! Instead, put it in a high interest savings account and earn interest on it, thus growing your net worth.

A lot of people have a problem with the idea of having money that they are not allowed to touch. My answer to every one of them has been this: rich people have it! They know the importance of net worth and having a large amount of money sitting in an account earning interest. The interest that you earn on this account is unearned income that can be passed down to your children, can be used for your child's college education, or portions of it can be used for trust funds.

It is alright to move your savings into other money making accounts like mutual funds or bonds, but just make sure that the investment vehicle you choose is safe. A mutual fund is a form of collective investment that pools money from many investors and invests the money in stocks, bonds, short-term money market instruments, and/or other securities.

No money is ever really "safe" but mutual funds are a relatively low risk way of investing your long-term savings. If you set up an account with a proven mutual fund, your money should be pretty safe.

You should not gamble with your savings. This means if you have $1,000 saved in a savings account, getting a government bond would be a safe bet to earn a return on that $1,000. It would not be wise to take that $1,000 and spend it all on lottery tickets. You also should not use this money to buy any particular stock in the stock market. With such volatile investments, you are more likely to lose money than accumulate wealth. I have an account designed for taking risks, so use your savings account for safe returns only.

Money to Burn: 10% of the extra money that is gained from proper budgeting should be allocated to a money-to-burn account. Of all the accounts, I am almost positive that this is going to be your favorite. Your money-to-burn account is to be spent on whatever you want it to be spent on. Strike that, the purpose of this account is to spend money solely on you. Your money-to-burn account is designed to reward yourself for a job well done.

Human beings are slightly hedonistic in nature so it is not reasonable to spend all of your time saving. Just like people who never save are in bad shape, people who always save run the risk of being in bad shape as well. There are countless examples of individuals who spend the bulk of their life saving money just to have a midlife crisis and blow their savings trying to recapture their youth. I do not want this to happen to you. And for that reason, I want you to make sure that you take 10% of your extra money and spend it doing something really nice for yourself.

If you have $200 extra after you have budgeted your money, you can take $20 of that and spend it on whatever you wish. You can take yourself out to see a movie. Go to the video store and buy a new DVD. Go to the shopping mall and buy something for yourself. It doesn't matter what you do with it, as long as you spend it on yourself—the more extravagant the better.

Even though this is free spending, there are a few rules with this account. The first rule is you have to spend all of it; yes all of it! At the end of the month, you must not have a penny left in your account. The second rule is, you must not take money from your other accounts to extend the amount you have to burn. This account as a reward to yourself. You shouldn't reward yourself for taking money out that is already allocated for other things. The third and final rule is you need to spend the money in this account as extravagantly as you can.

When I first started this program I didn't have that much money to blow. I would be lucky if I had $10 to use at the end of the month. So at the end of the month, I would add $10 to my food budget and order something that I usually couldn't afford at a restaurant. After about two months of following this program, I decided that I wanted to do something more extravagant than ordering a steak. The next month, I worked really hard and had about $90 in my money-to-burn account. I took that $90 and hired a private violinist to serenade my girlfriend for an hour in a park. The next month, I was determined to do something even more extravagant. At the end of that month, I had about $150 in my money-to-burn account. With that money, I went base jumping for the first time. I have since done more extravagant things.

More importantly, because my money-to-burn account has grown larger, all of my other accounts reap the benefits of my desire to try new things. This is because in order to have more money in this account, I have to make more money overall. And because I make more money overall, all of my budget categories have more in them. See, sometimes your desire for adventure can be a positive thing.

Preparing to Manage Millions

Education: 10% of the extra money that you have left over should be allocated to your personal education. Just because some people believe that education isn't important doesn't mean that they are right! To educate yourself means that you are trying to better who you are and the life that you are living. And for that reason, you should have some money allocated to help with your education.

When I talk about education, I am not just talking about tuition. Of course, part of this fund could be used for that, but that is not the purpose of this account. This account should be used for other forms of education. Have a hobby that you love? Well, take some classes or get some private instructions on how to do your hobby more efficiently. Do you play an instrument? Take the money in this account to take an advanced lesson. Spend the money on some form of non-academic education. I had a friend who used the money in his education account to get over his fear of public speaking. As a result of that investment, he is speaking professionally and is the happiest he has ever been.

Your education is your most important investment. Learning new techniques and proven systems will help you do many things more efficiently. Some of the smartest people in the world spend large amounts of money taking lessons from other people. They are always attending innovative seminars, buying new books, or joining a new program so that they can do their job that much better. This is what I am advising you to do. Take the time and the effort to explore new things. Your talents and happiness will grow exponentially as a result.

Philanthropy: 10% of the extra money that you have from budgeting like a Financial Antermologist should be used for philanthropy. It always feels great to give to the less fortunate. It is also a great thing to help those who are in need. This account should be created to feed your conscience. There is something inherently good about being able to donate to other people. No matter who you are, giving feels great when you give to those who deserve it.

You can give money to a homeless person on the street or to a church organization. You can donate money to the Red Cross or your political party of choice. You can donate money to friends and family or you could start a scholarship fund in your name. It's entirely up to you. Just make sure that you give.

In some instances, giving can also serve as a tax write-off. This is great for you because it means you will have more money in your pocket at the end of the year. Now, I'm not saying to give money for the soul purpose of being able to deduct it on your taxes; but it is still nice to know that there are added advantages to your decision to give.

Savings and Investments: 10% of the extra money that you have should be used for saving and investments. Remember how I advised you not to take risks with your long-term savings? Well, this is the budget category designed for you to take risks. This category allows you to take your money and have it work for you. The result could be a new revenue stream that could potentially allow you to earn residual income for the rest of your life. Or, it could offer you a short return on your money from unexpected places.

I caught my first real break with my investment account when a friend of mine came to me with a problem. He was looking into purchasing new equipment for his start-up business but did not have the collateral to secure a loan. Not many people or institutions like banks would have loaned him the money for his idea, but I liked his passion and decided that I would take the risk. In exchange for my investments, we agreed that I would claim a 15% stake in the profits generated from the company. Even I couldn't believe what happened next. I had moved on to other things and checked in occasionally on how his business idea was going. He was always honest with me and told me when things were going slow and when they were really speeding up.

About 21 months into operating his business, he landed a contract with Wal-Mart to carry the product that he developed. As a result, his order volume has multiplied 300 times over and he is flourishing. More importantly, I still have a 15% stake in every dime that he has made up to this point.

I reinvest the money that I earn from his idea into my advanced budgeting categories. I am able to pay for trips, invest money in other companies and even invest in myself. And this was all the result of a $2500 investment risk. Situations like this do not always happen, but I am living proof that they indeed do.

And you may not run across the next million dollar idea, but literally millions of investment opportunities become available every day and your long-term investment account will put you in a position to help someone develop their next great idea. This is especially important while you are in college. Think about how many aspiring students come up with great ideas for a student-run company. Now think about how many great ideas get scrapped because the student doesn't have the start-up capital.

This could very well be your ticket. I made the smart choice to invest in a few good ideas in college and they have panned out. I was really ahead of the curve because no other students had an investment account available to supply student entrepreneurs with money.

Preparing to Manage Millions

Now that you know that success can come from investing in others, it's time for you to start putting money into your savings and investment accounts!

Necessities: Your necessities account should account for 50% of the money left over after paying your bills. Your necessities account should be used to expand your emergency fund: 20%-30%. The rest of the money in your necessities fund should be used on whatever you feel is necessary. It all depends on what you would like to do with the surplus.

Depending on how much money you save every month, this account can get quite large. I had one friend have his necessities account shoot up to $5,000 in 11 months! His account was high because he was determined to budget the best that he could so that he would have large amounts of money in his advanced budgeting accounts.

You should determine how much money you will need for necessities. I don't think that it is necessary to have more than $1000 of emergency funds on hand while you are in college. Of course, if you want to have more or less, that is perfectly fine, but $1,000 is a good number. Once you get to that point, you can use the money that you would have put in this account to save for anything that you want. Let me give you an example from my life.

When I was in high school I really wanted my own 88 key Roland grand keyboard. I have a great interest in music and have been playing the piano for more than a decade. At the time, the only thing I wanted was a brand new piano. Since I had about $1,000 in my necessities account, I started saving for the piano. It cost about $550 at the time. I looked back at my budget, searching for ways to   reduce my financial obligations. There wasn't much I could really get rid of since I was only obligated to spend about $275 a month on bills, food, and transportation.

Preparing to Manage Millions

The only result was to find another source of income. This is where I came up with the idea to write my first book. It wasn't a Harry Potter hit, but it got the job done. I went to my school library and pulled up all the information I could about the history of my school. I wrote a 50-page pamphlet on the dark side of my school and past administrators. I printed the books and sold them for $5 each. The books cost about $2 to make. Because I needed to make $1,100 ($550 for my necessities and $550 divided evenly among my other accounts; that's right no shortcuts!), I had to sell 367 copies in order to get the piano that I wanted.

It took me about three months, but I met my goal and was able to buy my piano. Along with the piano, I was able to add $110 to my savings, money to burn, philanthropy, education, and long-term investment budget categories. I was able to buy myself 15 new songbooks with $55 and used the other $55 to go to a concert with money from my "money to burn" account. I set aside $75 to my graduation fund and gave $35 from my philanthropy fund to a friend who couldn't afford to pay his graduation fund.

I paid $100 for two sessions with a piano virtuoso who taught me some very useful skills that I still use today. I was able to do that with the money in my education account. And I was able to put $110 into my savings account (which I still haven't spent), and I loaned a friend $110 from my investments account to help pay for a new saxophone. He wanted the saxophone so that he could do private shows.

As a result of the budgeting program, my drive to get a piano also allowed me to afford a lot of extra things. I have repeated this same process many times and, as a result, have accumulated a large emergency fund and a large savings account; In addition, I have a lot of money currently working for me in my long-term investment account, which will give me more money to add to each one of these advanced budget accounts. And this does not include the money that I actually make from working! Can you believe that it all started with me dividing up 10 extra dollars a month?

Conclusion

Being able to budget like a Financial Antermologist will open more doors for you than you could ever dream of. If you adopt the advanced budgeting techniques that I outlined, you will be well on your way to financial freedom. It may be slow at first, but after a few weeks, or a month or two, you will start to see positive results in each of your accounts. And as you see your numbers grow, you will be inspired to make more money so that you will be able to put more money in them. The more money that you make, the more money you are able to save. Better yet, the more money you make, the more you will be able to burn!

Making money and budgeting does not have to be boring. If you put yourself on a solid plan, make fun goals for yourself, and find creative ways to execute your plan, making money and budgeting will be a blast. I wanted to put

Budgeting does not have to be boring!

more money into my advanced budgeting accounts, so I started three businesses and realized my dream of becoming a professional speaker. And all of this happened before I was 21! If this isn't fun, I don't know what is.

I have gone to great lengths to outline the budgeting process and why it should be important in your life. I hope you take the concepts and advice that I have given to heart and start using the tools that you have learned immediately. The quicker you start, the quicker you will be on your way to financial freedom. In reading this book, you have taken the first steps to being actively involved in your financial future. Don't let it end at just reading a few chapters; get out there and start budgeting with the concepts I've outlined here. I believe in you, I know you believe in yourself; now let's get out there and start you on your freedom path!

Review

1. Throwing away the money you saved through proper budgeting is a waste of time.

2. Use your extra money to create advanced budget categories to challenge yourself to be a well-rounded person.

3. Long-term savings should never be spent.

4. Educating yourself is the single most important investment you will ever make.

5. Giving is great.

6. Don't be afraid to invest in a great idea; it may turn out to be your meal ticket.

7. If anyone tells you that budgeting isn't fun, they just aren't doing it right!

Review Questions

1. What are the six advanced budget categories and what percentage should be allocated to each?

2. What are some of the safest places to put your long-term savings?

3. Let's say you have $1,000 in your necessities account and you just won $900 at bingo, what would you do with your winnings?

Chapter 7

What Happens When You Get Into Trouble

"One of the true tests of leadership is the ability to recognize a problem before it becomes an emergency."
-Arnold H. Glasgow

No matter how efficiently you budget or how far you plan ahead, there will always be trouble. Whether there is some unexpected emergency or an unplanned expense, there will be a time when you will have a need for emergency cash. Whether it is a big or small emergency, they will still require money that you already have budgeted for something else.

Even though you may get into a jam, it doesn't mean that you will have to abandon your budget to pay for the emergency. You have worked too hard to let a hiccup get in your way. Instead, let's spend this chapter discussing some ways in which you can work through your problem without ruining your budget. In this chapter, I discuss how to use an emergency fund, where to find some extra money, as well as the wrong places to get money to ease your financial troubles. Let's first take a look at emergency funds.

Emergency Fund

Your emergency fund was established for the sole purpose of being your first line of defense when in a financial bind. It was designed to help you through any emergency situation. Having your own emergency fund will save you from having to borrow money from friends or family; it will also prevent you from having to pay interest on an emergency loan. Whether it is $20 or $2,000, your emergency fund will be your first line of defense when trouble comes.

You should keep enough money in your emergency fund to cover three to six months of expenses. Don't worry if you can't do it all at once; an emergency fund can be built over time. So where does your emergency fund come from? Your emergency fund is actually a part of the necessities budget category that we set up in the previous chapter. You should allocate 20%-30% of your necessities account to your emergency fund.

To put it into perspective, allow me to provide a quick example. Let's say you have $500 at the end of the month to divide among your advanced budget categories: $250 (50% for necessities) will go into your necessities account. Of that $250, $50-$75 will go into your emergency fund. Depending on how you set up the allocation of your budget accounts (separate vs. central accounts), your emergency fund should be kept separate from your necessities fund. If using a separate account structure, you can open up a simple savings account. If using budgeting software, all you need to do is add another category folder for your emergency fund.

You deserve to be your own guardian angel. You have taken so much time and patience to budget properly; I would advise you to use this fund first before taking any other action. And it is okay if you clean out your emergency fund. If that is the case don't fret about it, just continue to put 20%-30% of your necessities account into your fund when you start over. If you choose to put more, that is fine as well.

Just make sure that you continue to put money into this account. If you fail to continue to save up for emergencies, you could find yourself in real trouble the next time an unexpected emergency happens.

Borrow from a Friend or Family Member

Sometimes the money in your emergency fund just isn't enough. If you are fortunate enough to have a friend or family member willing to help you through your trouble, you should capitalize on the opportunity. Just make sure to put together a repayment plan. Some will be relaxed about repayment; others will expect their money back on a certain date. You might be fortunate enough to have someone that will not ask for payment at all. Lucky You!

Whatever the repayment schedule, you must come up with a plan to get the money back. Maybe you will pay back the entire amount when you receive your next paycheck—this will probably throw off some of the numbers in your budget—but at least you are not stuck with owing someone money. Just make sure you have enough to cover your recurring expenses for the month.

If you choose to pay it back at a later date, it may be wise to take out equal portions from the next couple of paychecks that you get. This way, you are not stuck with one huge financial burden at the time of repayment.

Getting a Loan

If you choose to get a loan, make sure you don't just get a loan from the first bank you find. Shop around for competitive rates and a repayment schedule that will fit your budget. Look for a bank that is hungry for new business and is offering some kind of incentive for banking with them.I personally only use a bank loan as a last resort. I do this because banks will charge you interest on the amount that you borrow from them and you will end up paying more money for this emergency than you necessarily should have. If you do get a loan, try to get a payment schedule that will let you pay it back as soon as you realistically can. The longer it takes to pay back the loan, the more you are going to have to pay in interest. We want to guard against that by taking out a loan with a quick repayment schedule.

I will show you in the second part of this book how to establish a strong relationship with banks. This will allow you to walk into a bank that you have a relationship with and easily get a loan for any amount.

What Not to Do

There are many places that you can go to access some extra cash to pay for an emergency. Conversely, there are many places in which you should not go to get an emergency loan. Here is a short list of the places in which you should not go if you need to get some quick cash.

- A Payday Loan Store

- A Loan Shark

- A Title Loan Store

Payday Loan Store: Most of these places are a scam from the word go. These places will agree to give you small loans that you must pay back in a short amount of time. The problem with these places is they charge very high interest rates; more interest than you should ever pay on any loan that you take out. I have heard of some payday loan stores that charge 150% (Yes 150!) interest on even the smallest loans. This means that if you take out a loan for $100, you would have to pay $250 to satisfy your obligation. Oftentimes they expect repayment in less than a month!

A large number of these companies are currently being sued for charging an astronomical amount of interest. As a result, some are lowering their interest rates. Even with the lowered interest rates, the interest charges are still too high for such a small loan. Most of the time, you will find yourself in more trouble after a payday loan than when you started. Save yourself the headache and stay away from payday loan establishments.

A Loan Shark

I don't think I really need to explain what is wrong with loan sharks. If you do not know what they are, it's almost good that you don't. A loan shark is an individual who operates much like a payday loan establishment. They will agree to give you a small (or large) loan and you have a finite time to repay it. There are usually no problems if you pay them back on time; the problems arise when you don't.

The difference between loan sharks and a payday loan store is a loan shark will not put nonpayment on your credit report. Usually loan sharks will not rest until they retrieve from you what they feel will settle the value they place on the loan. This means they will oftentimes come into your home and take your personal possessions.

Back in the early 1900s, loan sharks were gangsters with connections to organized crime and were not hesitant to "disappear" someone if a loan was not repaid. The world has changed a bit since then, but loan sharks are still people you do not want to have to deal with. They can threaten you and will use any measure they can to try and get their money back. You do not need that kind of stress in your life.

Stay away from loan sharks! If they are not your personal friend, a family member, or a friend of the family, stay away from their offers.

A Title Loan Store

A title loan store operates much like a payday loan facility. The major difference is title loan stores usually require the surrender of an asset as a personal guarantee. Title loan establishments usually have you turn over the title to your car as a personal guarantee. You don't need me to tell you what happens if you default on a title loan.

Title loan facilities also charge a moderately high interest rate on the loans that they give out. These types of loans are usually reserved for individuals who need short term cash and are willing to pay extra for the convenience of having a little extra money today. Payday or title loans should never be a long-term option for dealing with emergencies.

A Freebie Just For You

As an alternative to dealing with a loan shark, I have another way in which you can get money for an emergency loan. The Hebrew Free Loan Society, located at 205 East 42nd St., New York, NY 10017, will make a loan to people in need - up to $800. There is no interest on the loan, and it is scheduled to be repaid over a period of one year. Two endorsers are needed. Write to them for complete details. I will show you how to easily get two endorsers in part two of this book.

Conclusion

Alright! I have covered several ways to obtain some emergency cash. This completes Part I of this book. Equipped with your newfound budgeting knowledge, you are way ahead of the budgeting curve. Honestly, many adults do not know the concepts that have just been introduced to you. If you apply the knowledge you have just acquired, you should be well on your way to achieving financial freedom.

Along with knowing how to budget, understanding the nuances of your credit report will take you a long way toward saving thousands in interest charges throughout your life. Part II will cover the basics of credit and how you can use your credit profile to your advantage.

Most adults don't learn this information in their lifetimes; it is a great advantage to you that you learn this information while in college.

If you don't have any objections, let's move to Part II.

Review:

1. Financial emergencies will occur at some point in your life; your emergency fund should be your first line of defense.

2. You should allocate 20%-30% of your necessities budget category to your emergency fund.

3. If your emergency requires more than what is in your emergency fund, try reaching out to family and friends.

4. Try getting a loan for the amount that you need, but stay away from payday loan establishments and loan sharks.

Review Questions:

1. How much, in terms of expenses, should be in your emergency fund?

2. What are some alternate sources of emergency cash?

3. When should you get a loan from a Title Loan facility?

PART II – Your Credit

Chapter 8

Why Is Your Credit Important?

"Debt is the slavery of the free."
-Publilius Syrus

As we enter into Part II of this book, I want to pause and give you a clear picture of why we are studying credit. Financial Antermologists have made it their mission to become proficient in the nuances of budgeting and credit because we understand the true power in understanding that the credit system influences almost all consumer transactions.

The techniques included in this book are the same techniques that I use to stay ahead of the credit curve. People may have told you that credit is what you use to get a house and a car and that credit is something that will either open doors or close all the right ones. While all of these are true, credit is more important than that. Your credit is something that will follow you for the rest of your life. Let me try my best to put credit into context.

Your Credit Report Is Your Official Financial Transcript.

Your credit report will greatly influence what kind of lifestyle you live. It is what will open up many opportunities for you and your family. With excellent credit, you can finance homes, the car of your dreams, and luxury items like boats and vacation homes. These kinds of opportunities will not be open to you if there are major blemishes on your credit report.

Have you ever wondered how individuals are able to afford multi-million dollar yachts or homes so large you run the risk of getting lost? I'll let you in on a secret. They are not paying cash for these items. For a very long time, I thought they were making so much money that they could just afford to flat out buy all of these luxury items. Instead, they use their strong credit report to finance these items and pay for them over several years, sometimes decades. This concept was very new to me when I was learning about credit, and I wanted to learn more.

In order to be able to live like successful Financial Antermologists, I found that you need to do two things: to be able to manage the money that you have, despite your income, and to have a credit profile that reflects that you are able to manage the income that you are making. Lucky for you, I taught you the former in Part I and I am teaching you the latter part of the equation in Part II. Many people learn the first part but fall short when they realize that making and managing money is only half the battle. And even if you do not land a job where you earn millions of dollars a year, using the budgeting techniques in Part I will give you enough financial discipline so that you can afford a lot of the luxury items you want.

Your credit report is designed to either exponentially help you or greatly burden you when it is time to make major life decisions. This is why budgeting is so important. If you know how to budget properly, you will be able to handle your finances in such a way that you do not damage your credit report. All of the strong budgeting attributes that you possess will show up on your credit report and it will prove to creditors who want to give you money to finance your dream items that you are a strong credit candidate. This is precisely what I want. I want you to have a credit profile that demonstrates that you are equipped to handle a high-priced item like a car or home.

This is not to say that I expect you to go out and buy a high-priced item. Instead, if you show that you can budget like a millionaire; most finance companies will treat you like one. Once you reach that point, the doors of the credit world will open up to you. Not only that, but you will end up saving thousands of dollars in your lifetime when creditors calculate finance charges. Let me explain why.

Whenever you get a loan, you are agreeing to accept money today with the promise that you will pay it back at a later date. As an added incentive, you agree to pay a little extra (interest) to help convince the lender to part with their money. In essence, for every dollar that you borrow today, you will pay back that original dollar plus a little more by the time you finish paying. This is how banks stay in business; it is in their best interest to safely loan out as much as they can. I must emphasize safely because lenders do their very best to make sure that they are lending their money to someone who is sure to pay them back. This is why your credit profile is important.

It should be noted that with the change in today's economy, the above statement should be qualified. As a result of banks not following the very practices that keep them in business, like giving out safe loans, the entire world is entering into a global recession. Those who thought that they had good credit in the past are finding it very difficult to find financing for even small items.

If you believe that now is not an important time to really make sure that you have your finances and credit report in dean's list shape, you are sadly mistaken.

Many people assume that your credit profile determines whether or not you will be approved for a loan. That is not entirely true. If you have terribly good or terribly bad credit, it is cut and dry whether or not you will be approved for a loan from a lender. If you are like the other 70% of Americans, you fall somewhere in the gray area between the two extremes.

This makes your credit report very important. Your credit report will determine whether or not you will be approved for the loan that you are attempting to get. More importantly, if you are approved for the loan, your credit report will determine how much interest you will have to pay when it is time to pay the loan back. The better your credit report, the less you will have to pay.

A Real World Example

I use this example in my seminars often because it is very effective. It truly highlights how having a strong credit profile is important, as well as demonstrates how starting sooner rather than later is very advantageous, especially if you are in college. Do you mind if I use you in this example? Thanks!

You and your best friend have just graduated from college and have landed a job that pays a great salary for a recent college graduate: $70,000 a year. You both are really excited because you were roommates and now you will be working the same job for the same company.

Before I continue, let me say this: the stated salary that you get is an illusion. You will never take that amount home. This is merely the amount the United States government will tax you for. If you are making $70,000 a year, you can count on old Uncle Sam taking at least 30% of that. So even though you tell your friends that you make $70,000 a year, you may only see $49,000. And of that $49,000, you still have to pay for healthcare, insurance, and possibly a retirement fund; so plan on taking home less than that! Depending on your current plan, you could actually only take home anywhere from $40,000 to $45,000 a year! I did not include this to deter you, I just thought that it was important that you know that your stated salary is not your take-home salary.

So, when you are putting together your annual budget once you get out of college; make sure to keep the concept of take-home salary in mind. This will give you a better idea of the amount of income you will have available to put into your budget categories. Ok, back to the example.

Now that you know what your salary will be, it is time for you to find a place to stay and a car to get you back and forth to work every day. You both decide that you all are going to get a place in the same neighborhood (but not live together, you both have had enough) and shop for a car at the same time. You were both strong students. The only difference between the two of you is that you have applied the concepts in this book to your current life and your roommate wouldn't take your advice and decided to wait and read the book once he graduated. You walk into the car dealership and you both choose the same car in different colors.

You both sit down with the dealer and he crunches the numbers. You both decide to finance about $25,000 for your cars and you choose a plan that allows you to have the entire loan paid off in 72 months. The dealer has both of your credit profiles in hand. In looking at your credit profile, he offers you an annual percentage rate (APR) of 6%. With a weaker profile, your roommate uses his savvy and talks him down to a 9% APR. Not a major difference right? It's only three percent.

Wrong! Because you had a 6% APR, your monthly payment is $313. With an APR of 9%, your roommate's monthly payment is $340. On the surface, this doesn't look like a big difference. If that is the case to you, you are only taking these numbers at face value. After 72 months, your roommate will have paid $2,000 more than you have for the exact same car! There was no difference in the performance or the price of the two vehicles. The only difference is one of you chose to budget and build your credit in college; the other didn't. Your roommate is fine with the price of his car and you both drive down to the local real estate company to look for a place to live.

The mortgage broker compliments you all on your cars then you drive around the city looking for a place to live. You both find the perfect neighborhood near the workplace and decide that you want to buy in the same building. It is a very nice building that just opened and they have two condominiums left. You both decide to act!

You drive back to the mortgage broker's office and he crunches the numbers. Neither of you have a down payment so you finance the entire amount. Each condo costs $150,000. You both take out a 30-year loan making payments on a monthly basis. He sits down at the desk and looks at both of your credit profiles. He is impressed with your profile, and as a result, gets a bank to finance your condominium at 7% APR. Your roommate tries to use his savvy with the mortgage broker but he doesn't budge. He gives your roommate a 15% APR. That doesn't sound like much more than yours, does it? You better believe it is!

A difference of 8% annually isn't a lot on short-term loans that aren't compounded often. With a 30-year mortgage loan, this 8% difference is compounded monthly for 30 years. The fact that it is compounded makes a huge difference.

As a result of working hard to budget properly and using part II of this book, your monthly payment for your condo is $998. Unfortunately for your late bloomer roommate, he is stuck with an $1897 monthly bill! If he chooses to live in this condo, it would drastically reduce his cash flow every month. At 7% annually you will end up paying $360,000 total for your $150,000 condominium.

Conversely, if your roommate chooses to purchase the condominium, he would pay a grand total of $682,798; a difference of more than $300,000. This is an identical condo in the same building!

> *To see how I got these numbers, you can log onto www.copocket.co to use one of the free calculators.*

There is no difference in the square footage of the two condos. The only difference is you decided to take an active role in your financial future early and your roommate decided to wait it out. And for that reason, he is stuck paying $300,000 more for the same square footage in the same building. **This Is Why Having A Strong Credit Report Is Important Sooner Than Later!**

Most don't believe that their credit is important just out of college. This example shows you that your credit report can have a very large effect on a lot of your finances. With higher rates, more of your money is being used to pay interest so you won't have the freedom to spend money on other things. It is my mission to make sure that you get the better rate instead of the rates that your roommate got. You must remember there is a high probability that you will have to pay back student loans along with other recurring expenses, so the less in interest you must pay, the better off you will be down the road.

I want you to succeed because I know you understand how important your financial future is. For that reason, I have gone through great lengths in Part II of this book to explain credit, demystify your credit profile, and show you an example of how someone can generate a strong credit profile on their own. With that strong profile, he is consistently offered the best interest rates.

Even with a strong credit profile, being fresh out of college puts you at a real disadvantage. For that reason, I have included several ways in which you can embellish your credit applications to help further convince creditors that you are a credit veteran.

With these useful tips, you will be able to finance items you would not have been able to until you were at least 30.I'm excited to expose the secrets Financial Antermologists use every day. Are you ready? It's time to continue!

Review

1. Your credit report is your official financial transcript.

2. Your annual salary is not the same as your take home salary. Expect your take-home salary to be at least 30% less than your stated salary.

3. The sooner you begin building a strong credit profile, the sooner you will start receiving premium rates on high-ticket items.

Review Questions

1. How does your credit profile help you in your everyday life?

2. What is the difference between your salary and your take-home pay?

3. Can you be passed over for a job or promotion because you have bad credit?

Chapter 9

Your Credit Profile: A Detailed Look

"Youth is in danger until it learns to look upon debts as furies."
-Edward G. Bulwer-Lytton

I want to take the time to examine credit profiles in more detail. I personally feel that in order to effectively master something, you definitely need to have a good understanding of how it works. For that reason, I am going to talk about the nuances of your credit report.

Unless you have your own business, there are really only three major credit bureaus that you should know about when you are thinking about credit. The three companies are Equifax, Experian, and TransUnion. They are the major bureaus that hold about 99% of the data that go into your credit history. Let's take a look at the details of your credit profile.

How To Get A Copy

Before I begin talking about what's in your credit report, it would be helpful to tell you how you can secure a copy of your own. Obtaining a copy of your credit report is relatively simple and there are a number of ways to do it. Some are easier and better than others though. Let's look at them now.

Visit Credit Bureau Sites: The simplest way to get a copy of your credit profile is to visit the website of each credit bureau and request a copy. Most of them will give you the opportunity to view your credit profile once for free. Beyond that, you will have to pay. Although they will let you see your profile, seeing your credit score will not be free.

Sign Up for a Credit Monitoring Service: While visiting each site directly is the simplest, using a credit reporting agency is probably the most convenient. When you sign up with a credit monitoring agency, they allow you full access to your credit report whenever you want it (not the scores though) and they even send you friendly emails to let you know if there has been any recent activity or changes to your credit report. This feature is very important nowadays because it gives you the opportunity to recognize if you are a victim of identity theft long before the thieves have a chance to do too much damage.

With identity theft being the fastest-growing crime in the world, it would not be a bad idea to have a watch on your credit profile for any unauthorized charges. Most credit monitoring services offer a free trial so that you can try out their service for 30 days. A monthly subscription is relatively inexpensive.

Trust me, $10 a month is a lot cheaper than the time, energy, and money you will spend if you find out six months too late that someone has stolen your identity.

Notice of Aversive Action: If you have ever applied for credit, insurance, or a job and have been denied due to your credit, the law requires that you receive a "notice of adverse action." In this notice, they outline why you were denied and they give you instructions on how you obtain a free copy of your credit report.

Although this is a free way to get a copy of your credit report, I personally do not feel it will be a wise way to obtain a copy. Here's why: whenever you apply for credit, there is an official inquiry (I'll explain later) that lands on your credit report. Inquiries have the potential to negatively damage your credit report if you have too many, so it would be wise to use the other two methods described above to get a copy of your report. If you do apply for credit and are denied, then using this method is an easy way to verify the information that they used to reject you.

Breakdown of Your Credit Report

Your official credit report is divided into four main sections: personal information, public records, credit history, and inquiries. Each section is very important and together they tell creditors just about everything they need to know about you as a person of credit. Let's look at each section in detail.

I want to note that although I am covering a good amount of detail about your credit report, there is a lot more to know and understand about your credit report and how your actions positively and negatively affect it. If you want to learn more, go to www.copocket.co and read more articles. Also, the site features an actual copy of a credit report so that you can see what will be covered in the next sections.

Personal information: The personal information section includes your name, address, date of birth, social security number, spouses' name, and your employer. Some credit reports also include former addresses and any former names that you may have gone by. Credit bureaus receive this information from creditors that report to the bureaus whenever you apply for credit.

Public Records: Public records are any liens, judgments, garnishments, bankruptcies, or felony convictions that you may have. Basically, anything that you may have had to go to court for can be put in this section.

This is a very important part of your credit report as it is frequently prone to errors. While this section doesn't always affect your credit score nearly as much as later sections, there are some things to watch out for. Bankruptcies on your credit report will greatly impact your score, as will judgments and liens. If you see any of these in error, make sure to contact the credit reporting agency and request that it be removed.

Credit History: Arguably the most important section of your credit report. This section gives a detailed account (7 years' worth) of your payment and nonpayment of debt. Items in this section include, but are not limited to, loans, mortgages, credit cards, and collection accounts. Along with each item, there is a timeline of your payment history and various details about the account.

For example, the details could include the name of the creditor, what type of account it is (ex. credit card, mortgage, etc.), the outstanding balance, and the credit limit. Your payment history is broken down into a series of numbers. I have included the numbers and their meanings below:

0. Too new to rate

1. Pays account as agreed

2. Not more than two payments past due

3. Not more than three payments past due

4. Not more than 4 payments past due

5. At least 120 days or more past due

6. Making regular payments under W.E.P (wage earner plan)

7. Repossession

8. *Bad Debt; placed for collection; skip*

Inquiries: This is a listing of every company who has requested a copy of your credit report. This section is usually divided into two sub sections: "hard" and "soft" inquiries. Hard inquiries are the result of you applying for credit. Whenever you apply for credit, a car, or mortgage loan, the finance company will pull a copy of your credit report. The result is a hard inquiry on your credit.

As I stated earlier, too many hard inquiries have a negative impact on your credit score; it gives the appearance that you are desperate for financing. Having more than two hard inquiries on your credit report can drop your credit score. To prevent this, try using a soft inquiry first to check your report and score yourself before you go shopping for financing.

A soft inquiry is the result of you pulling your own report or a third party company pulling your report to market their products to you (credit card offers). These are only seen by you and do not impact your credit score.

How Long Do Items Stay On Your Report

Bankruptcies remain on your credit report for 10 years. Any other negative item remains no longer than 7 years from the date of the first delinquency. If you have something positive on your credit report, it can remain indefinitely, but no less than ten years. Inquiries remain on your report for two years. If you have applied for credit in the last 6 months, they will
be given more consideration and impact your score more than hard inquiries after 6 months.

Your Credit Score

Most times, a credit score is provided when you get a copy of your report. If not, they are available for an extra charge. There are two types of scores. The FICO score, also referred to as the "Beacon" score, is the industry standard for credit scores. It is the most valued score by creditors. It is calculated by the Fair Isaac company using data contained in your credit report.

The second type of score is the one provided by the credit reporting agencies themselves. Each agency has its own formula, so expect each score to be different. The three scores from the credit reporting agencies can be referred to as the TransUnion score, Experian Credit Expert score, and CreditXpert (Equifax). Because each formula is different, and sometimes vary greatly from one another, most creditors only use the FICO score provided by Fair Isaac.

Conclusion

It is truly important to have a "paying on time" history. While having one or two late payments will not ruin your credit, making consistent late payments (even a few days late) can negatively impact your credit in ways that can take years to truly recover from. Remember, credit reports hold seven years of history, so any mistakes that you make in your freshman year of college will still be on your credit report when you are 25...yikes!

This is why I spent so much time going over the importance of creating an effective budget in the first part of this book. It is designed to ensure that you only purchase what you can afford and, if you ever do run into trouble, you have some safeguards in place to make sure that you are not late paying back debts. While it may have been ok a few years ago to have a not-so-great credit score, with the economic trouble that the entire world is finding itself in, creditors are truly tightening their wallets and only giving to those with a proven track record of repayment.

So what might that mean for you? That means that when you get out of school and want to purchase your first condo or car, you will find it hard to get financing. I have also heard reports of individuals who let their credit slip in school and then got passed over for a job that they really wanted. I know this sounds extreme, but I have seen it happen. These are just some things to ponder the next time you are thinking about using your charge card, or better yet, applying for a new one.

I am glad that we have taken the time to go over what is in your credit report. Hopefully that has demystified credit for you. If it hasn't, the next two chapters will help. Let's move on to the differences between good and bad credit.

Review

1. The three major credit reporting agencies are Equifax, Experian, and Transunion.

2. You can obtain a copy of your credit report by going to an agency's website or through a credit monitoring service.

3. Bankruptcies stay on your credit report for 10 years and other negative information remains for 7 years.

4. FICO scores are the industry standard credit score and are provided by Fair Isaac.

5. It is important to not make late payments and not apply for credit unless you need it as they both negatively impact your credit score

Review Questions

1. Of all the credit scores, which is the most important and why?

2. How many hard inquiries does it take to negatively impact your score? Which carry more weight?

3. Can being convicted of a felony show up on your credit report?

4. You made a mistake and ran up a high credit card bill when you were 18 and stopped making payments; at what age will that negative mark leave your report?

Chapter 10

Good vs. Bad Credit

"We often pay our debts not because it is only fair that we should, but to make future loans easier."
-François de La Rochefoucauld

Depending on the credit bureau, credit scores range from 300-850. At what number do you think excellent credit begins? If you said 720, you are absolutely right! If you didn't, it's alright; most individuals go most of their adult lives not knowing their own number, let alone what number constitutes excellent credit. Here is what the numbers should mean to you.

If you are below 520, lenders will consider you a credit risk and will most often deny credit to you unless you can bring them a credit worthy co-signer. If you score between 520 and 720, you are considered a provisional borrower. This means you may or may not be granted credit; it all depends on the strength of your credit profile, the strength of your credit references, and other individual factors that lenders take into consideration. Just getting out of college, it is highly unlikely that you will reach the 720 mark unless you know what it takes to generate a great credit score.

I personally don't feel you should have to wait until you are 28-30 to enjoy the benefits of great credit. It is why I wrote this book. The way to good credit is not hard. It just takes dedication to sticking with your financial plan. This doesn't mean that maintaining good credit is easy either; it just means that you must remain active in your finances. This concept should be nothing new to you by now. When taking the time to develop an efficient budget, it will not be hard to master the discipline of maintaining a strong "paying on time" credit profile.

In this chapter, I show you the ins and outs of good and bad credit and how easy it is to get and maintain good credit. I also show you the advantages and disadvantages of having both. At the end of this chapter, I hope to convince you to further dedicate yourself to maintaining a strong credit profile. Let's start!

Good Credit

Believe it or not, attaining good credit is remarkably easy. It's not a matter of luck or how much money you earn. Having a good credit profile is the same as having a good transcript in school. Learn how to make the

> *The hardest part about credit is making sure that you keep your credit report clean and private.*

grade and you will excel. You just need to know the proper grades that you must earn on your credit report to generate substantial growth to your credit score.

The great part about your financial report card is that there is very little studying involved in order to excel. Applying the concepts that you learn in this book will put you well on your way to creating a top-notch credit report. It is all in the execution. There are no tests, no late night cramming sessions.

You can build your profile at your own pace with either a little effort or a lot. The more effort you put forth in the beginning, the better your profile will be when you are out of college.

When talking about good credit, there are many things that come to mind. How do I get a strong profile? Which types of credit are the best to get? If I miss a payment, is my credit ruined? All of these are very good questions. And if you have them, it shows that you really want to learn the nuances of credit. Let's look at some of these questions in detail.

How do I get a Strong Credit Profile? The secret to a strong credit profile is paying your bills on time and developing relationships with banks that will serve as strong credit references when it is time to apply for major credit.

What type of credit is the best credit to get? The best kind of credit to have on your credit profile by far is unsecured bank loans. Loans are the Holy Grail of showing creditors that you are able to pay back your debt in a timely fashion. This is because banks use tougher criterion to approve someone for a loan than a credit card company or a smaller creditor. For that reason, when a creditor sees that you have a series of bank loans paid off, it not only shows that you are credit worthy, it shows that you are a mature applicant that a bank can trust. When dealing with most creditors, that is more than good enough.

If I miss a payment is my credit report ruined? I used to think that this was the case. Missing a few payments will not ruin your credit, but it will not be a positive addition, either. Try to avoid this at all costs.

Establishing and maintaining good credit will open up many doors for you in the future. Did you know that there are vacations, travel deals, and other amenities only available to people with a credit rating over 750? I didn't know that until I was talking to an expert on the advantages of good credit.

Not only do you get access to a lot of things considered off limits, but you do not pay as much for the items that you would normally need credit for when you have a great credit score. These advantages are within your reach. All you need to do is create a well-balanced credit profile that incorporates a combination of bank loans, credit cards, and other types of credit accounts. Once creditors see that you are a well-rounded applicant, they will be more than willing to lend you money at lower rates. This is my goal for you.

Bad Credit

Bad credit is very easy to get as well. All you have to do is become relaxed about your repayment regiment, apply for the wrong kinds of credit, and/or flat out miss payments.

The only problem is that this behavior will cost you hundreds of thousands of dollars in your lifetime. You will have higher interest rates. You will be denied more often for the loans that you need. Financing something like a boat or a luxury vehicle will be out of the question. The credit card companies will make a small fortune from the interest charges that you accrue. You will be buried deep in debt with very few avenues to save you from the astronomical interest charges that you are paying.

This is not what you want for your life. This is not what I want for your life! Putting yourself in a bad credit situation will lead you down the same path of millions of Americans who fork out their hard-earned money paying interest to creditors. I believe that your money should be spent on a better cause: yourself! It is why I teach seminars on financial responsibility. It is why I help people just like you build a strong credit profile every day. It is why I am talking to you right now! Let's get you great credit.

Review

1. Credit scores range from 300-850 with a great score starting at around 720.

2. If your credit score is 520 or below, it is very likely that you will be turned down for most major forms of credit.

3. The difference between good credit and great credit is your dedication to maintaining your credit profile.

4. Getting great credit entails paying your bills on time and having a good credit mix.

5. Getting bad credit is easy if you consistently make late or even miss payments. Not having the money to cover your recurring expenses will allow this to happen sooner rather than later.

Review Questions

1. What is the range for credit scores?

2. How do you get good credit?

3. How do you get bad credit?

4. What are some of the advantages of having good credit?

Chapter 11

9 Credit Misconceptions Every Person
Should Know the Truth About.

"Some people use one half their ingenuity to get into debt, and
the other half to avoid paying it."
-George D. Prentice

The only clear thing about credit is that banks make billions of dollars a quarter making sure you are unclear about the rules of credit. I hate to make it sound like the people that work for this system are bad people. In fact, I'm pretty sure that most of them are pretty nice. But even nice people make deals with the devil. And for most, the credit system is Satan himself.

With the mountains of information that you are bombarded with when applying for credit, 30-page-long credit card forms, words you don't understand, rules that you don't learn about until they cost you money, there are a large number of people who don't have the slightest clue about what to do when it comes to credit. In doing research on consumer understanding of credit, my team found droves of individuals who receive misinformation about how the credit system works.

In this chapter, I have put down the nine most important credit misconceptions and have taken the liberty to include the truth. I hope it clears up some of the thoughts you had about credit so we can move forward from here with a newfound belief that you can take on the credit system and win.

Misconception # 1- *Credit Bureaus have authority granted to them by the government.*

This statement is absolutely false. Credit Bureaus are not empowered by any government authority. In fact, there are more laws protecting you from credit bureaus than there are laws protecting the credit bureaus. Let me tell you the truth about credit bureaus.

Credit bureaus are private companies. They are businesses that are designed to make money like any other company. The only difference is they sell your personal information to creditors looking to give you money. It is not a government entity; all three of the major credit bureaus are actually publicly traded on the New York Stock Exchange! The only government authority a credit bureau has over you is the right to sue in an attempt to collect money that is owed to them. But this right is guaranteed to citizens as well as companies.

Misconception # 2- *It is impossible to get bankruptcy off of your credit report.*

Where there is a will, there is a way. When it comes to credit reports, nothing is impossible. It is very possible for someone to steal your identity and put things that you never thought could be financed on your credit report. I was in Tampa, Florida attending a seminar and a very nice young lady I met was telling me about her battle with identity theft.

You will not believe what she found on her credit report! Apparently, she bought a puppy online for her little sister for Christmas and some very bad people got a hold of her information. When she went to check her credit report in March, she found that there were 6 puppies, 18 cats, 2 ponies, and an emu all financed on her credit report. She was a good sport by this time and we had a great laugh about it, but identity theft is very serious. I mean honestly, who finances an emu?

Anyhow, I digress. I told you that story to give you an example of someone who was able to have some really obscure things removed from her credit report. When it comes to bankruptcy, it is also very possible to get it taken off of your credit report. It is possible to get almost anything removed from your credit report.

Misconception # 3- *The information on your credit report will remain there unchanged forever.*

I used to think that this was true for a long time. First, information on your credit report changes monthly. Credit bureaus input new activity into your credit report all the time. When you pay your bills every month, the information is added to your credit report.

Also, because credit bureaus can only store a finite amount of your credit transactions, whenever something new gets added, the older entries start to fall by the wayside. Credit bureaus usually track your last 7 years of credit history, so if you have had credit for 15 years, everything from the first 8 years of your credit history no longer appear on your credit report. This may be a good or bad thing depending on how well you manage your credit.

You also don't have to wait 7 years for information to be taken off of your credit report. If there are errors on your credit report, it is possible to have it removed. I used to believe, once bad credit, always bad credit. I also used to believe that if there was a mistake on my credit report, the system would not allow me to have it taken off unless I had a court order or something. Truthfully, information on credit reports are changed all the time;

and it happens for more reasons than you think.

Credit bureaus have entire divisions devoted to correcting errors on credit reports. Granted, they do not always happen in the timeliest fashion, but they do occur. If there are any mistakes on your credit report, you can write a formal declaration to have the information changed and the credit bureau must investigate the inquiry. If they cannot find just cause for the incorrect marking to be there, by law, they must remove it from your credit report.

Credit bureaus do not like lawsuits or spending millions of dollars settling out of court. As a result, they usually make an attempt to verify an invalid marking on your credit report. This process usually takes no more than 15 business days.

Misconception #4 - *It is illegal or immoral to have entries on your credit report altered or removed.*

Not only is it legal, but it is very wise to do so. Why should you have to suffer because of someone else's actions? No human is perfect and we are all very prone to mistakes. There have been instances where individuals have made on-time payments for twenty years, just to check their credit and see that the creditor made a key stroke error and sprinkled in a few late payments on their credit report. The late payment stayed on their credit report for years and it continued to drag down their credit score. Their credit report suffered because late payments over longer periods of time on a credit report bring down the credit score because it signifies an inconsistent on-time payment history.

Because of that error, the person appeared to be more of a credit risk than they really were. You should check your credit report, at the minimum, once a year to check for inconsistencies. If you find any, it is your obligation to make sure that it gets changed so that it doesn't negatively impact your credit report down the line.

Misconception # 5- *Paying old past due debt removes it from your credit report.*

Your credit report gives the history of months, even years of credit transactions. If you are late making a payment, it will show up on your credit report. This isn't like school; you don't get half or full credit for turning in a late assignment. It will show up on your credit report card and stay there even after you have paid back the past due debt.

Let's say for example you were 10 days late making a payment in June of 2006. Even though you have since paid the past due debt, the next time you look at your credit report, you will see that under June 2006, there will be a note that says something to the effect of "late payment." And even though every month after that has been paid on time, creditors will still be able to see the blemish on your record.

I strongly advise that you try your best to make all of your payments on time. I say that because it only takes a few late payments on your credit report to make it seem as if you are a credit risk; which leads to higher interest rates. At this point in the development of your financial career, you really do not need the extra stress of paying a higher interest rate and/or appearing as if you are more of a credit risk than a young adult already is.

Misconception #6 - *Inquiries and checking your credit are not derogatory and will not affect your credit standing.*

Inquiries are the sore thumb of credit ratings. Whenever someone checks your credit, it shows up as an inquiry on your credit report. When you are applying for credit, you want to make sure that you are going to be approved so you would not mind having as many people checking your report as you can so that you can ensure you will be approved. Unfortunately, credit bureaus think that multiple inquiries in a short amount of time are not a good thing; ergo your credit score suffers.

If you do comparison shop for a rate, make sure to keep all of the inquiries in a short time frame, no more than 14 days. Otherwise it will seem as if you are looking for quick access to cash instead of comparison shopping for a loan. You get credit card offers in the mail all the time. Most of the time you receive these offers because a company has looked at your credit score without your knowledge. Any company under the sun will offer you a credit card when they inquire about your credit score. When you are just establishing your credit, you will receive offers from credit card companies that are more lenient with their requirements. These types of inquiries are actually sold to the credit card companies by the credit bureaus.

These credit cards typically charge a higher interest rate. Once you start to build your credit, the companies that will inquire will be the more established companies that will be willing to offer you gold and platinum cards. The only good thing about these inquiries is that they are treated differently on your credit report. You are not penalized if there are more than 100 soft inquiries on your credit report.

A word of advice: There have been instances where the miscellaneous credit offering by a company is interpreted by the credit bureau as a legitimate business requesting your information per your request. This happens to possibly three out of five people who have credit in the United States. If this ever happens to you, I advise you not to fret about it unless there are a significant number of false inquiries.

Credit companies do not like being bothered about excessive mistakes on credit reports because they honestly do not make money correcting such errors. So make sure there at least three or more false inquiries before you write the credit bureaus requesting that they remove the excessive number of inquiries from your credit report.

Misconception #7 - *If you get a derogatory item removed, it will show up again on your credit report.*

If a derogatory mark on your credit has been legally removed, by law it is not allowed to show up again on your credit report. If it does, you have cause to contact a lawyer and make a case against the credit bureau. I don't think that it will ever get to that point because credit bureaus are more than willing to take derogatory marks off and leave them off because they do not want to be sued.

Misconception # 8- *What you have done in the past reflects your credit future.*

This is a statement that I believed for years. When it comes to credit, time will allow for many changes in your credit profile. Your credit could be in top shape one day, but 6-8 months later, after being
laid off from work, you could find yourself with a lowered score from inability to make payments. Your credit profile is as fickle as anything else in the world. It can put you in a positive position one day and leave you in financial despair six months later.

There are literally millions (yes millions!) of Americans who make mistakes in college. They take out a few credit cards and end up leaving college with a couple thousand dollars in credit card debt. Adding student loan payments to credit card payments could put someone fresh out of college in a real predicament. As a result, millions fall behind on their payments. This does not mean they will be destined for financial failure.

Almost 60% of those who fall behind after college bounce back. And luckily, if you ever find yourself in this situation, it is very possible to bounce back. There have been plenty of individuals who have worked through their financial troubles and now have great credit. This is something that is absolutely within your reach.

Bad markings on your credit report from college mistakes almost become irrelevant if you can establish seven years of strong credit history after graduating. This is the long and hard way to go about getting past blemishes; the easiest way to work past blemishes is to guard against them in the first place. You have to learn to budget efficiently and make sure to constantly adjust your plans to fit your current situation.

Misconception #9 - Getting a Lawyer or Hiring a Credit Counselor is the Best Way to Go About Building and Maintaining your Credit.

Listen closely: the best person to build and maintain your credit is you! It is alright to have someone help you, but it is necessary for you to acquire this knowledge and do it on your own. The skills that you are learning in this book are absolutely necessary for every person. At the end of the day, if your lawyer makes a mistake, it is not his credit that is affected. As a matter of fact, whether he makes a mistake or not, he will still be paid for the work that he has done. And lawyers charge astronomical fees for something you can do yourself. Why would you pay $150 for something that will take you about 20 minutes to do on your own for free? It is absolutely not worth it.

Credit repair companies are also companies that you should not seek out when you are trying to work on your credit. This is not to say that you shouldn't go see a credit counselor. But understand that a credit counselor is different from a credit repair agency. A credit counselor will not charge you for the advice that they give. Credit repair agencies will. Credit repair companies are a scam from the word go. Most promise you spectacular results for a just a small fee and when they are done, your credit will be spotless. If you believe that statement you should believe this one:

"The second that you finish reading this book, the pages will automatically tear themselves away from the cover and plant themselves in the ground. You should water the ground every day because they possess the magic formula to create a money tree. Give it about 6-8 weeks and you will have a full grown tree full of one-hundred dollar bills!"

A credit repair agent does not have any special powers and cannot repair your credit any more efficiently than you can. The majority of credit repair agencies are scams that promise you great results and do little if any work at all. Most of them will spend money on marketing, get as many people to trust them as they can, then run away with all the profits! It is absolutely not worth it.

Instead, take the concepts that you have learned and will continue to learn from this book and put your financial future in your own hands. Take an active role in boosting, maintaining, and repairing your credit. If for no other reason, do it because I guarantee you are the only person who will have to deal with the consequences whether they are positive or negative.

When you outsource this responsibility, you will have someone sharing your positive consequences and will be alone if you have negative consequences. Why not do it on your own and keep the positive outcome for yourself?

Conclusion

I hope that clearing up these misconceptions have helped you gain a better understanding of credit and credit bureaus. If you are still confused, don't worry. This is the just the beginning. I devote an entire chapter to credit and how you can use credit bureaus to help you get everything you have ever dreamed of.

Let's continue.

Review

1. Credit bureaus do not have government authority; they are private companies traded on the New York Stock Exchange.

2. It is possible to have almost anything removed from your credit report, especially incorrect derogatory entries.

3. Paying back old debt doesn't erase it from your credit report.

4. Excessive soft inquiries are fine; excessive hard inquiries are bad news.

5. Previous mistakes do not mean that your credit is ruined forever. Millions of people have bounced back from mistakes made in college.

Review Questions

1. Which branch of government does the major credit reporting agencies belong to?

2. What can't be removed from your credit report? 3. True or False: Removing inaccurate information from your credit report is illegal?

3. If you pay back past due debt, does it remove the past due markings from your credit report?

Chapter 12

Establishing Credit: A Hypothetical Example

"The surest way to establish your credit is to work yourself into the position of not needing any."
-Maurice Switzer

One of the most important things you can do in college, on top of getting a good education, is establishing a strong financial foundation that includes good credit. Unfortunately, as we know, very few colleges in the United States actually teach students how to build that foundation. I have helped countless people build their own financial foundations and personal credit. Every year, I find that thousands of people are hungry for more credit knowledge.

I would like to share an example with you of a fellow Financial Antermologist and his method for building his own credit. It must be noted that this example is not to be consider legal or credit advice and should not be interpreted as such. It is included in this book only as an example of how a past student took the knowledge from this book and proactively started building their personal credit. Ok, on to the example. For privacy purposes, I will call the Antermologist "Scot.". Scot attended one of my seminars in early 2007. He had a ton of questions and was very interested in how he could start building his credit.

In my credit seminars, I include a section on what individuals can do today to get their credit score into the 700s in a matter of months and Scot took copious notes. Nine months later, I received a letter from him telling me that in 6 months, his credit rating grew from 480 to 740. I have included the method he used below.

The Set Up

Scot started his credit building journey with $1,000. He went on Google and conducted a search for local banks around his school. With a list of more than twenty, he called every bank and told them that he was interested in opening a savings account and wanted to ask them some questions. He chose three banks based on the answers they gave. I have included the questions that he asked below.

· *What is the minimum amount you must deposit for a passbook savings account?*

> A passbook savings account is a type of savings account where deposits and withdrawals are recorded in a small passbook that the bank will give you.

· *What is the minimum amount you can loan on a passbook savings account?*

· *How much of my passbook savings account can I borrow against?*

For the purpose of his plan, Scot was only interested in opening up an ordinary passbook savings account. He chose three banks that offered the highest interest rates on their savings account. More importantly, he based his decision on which banks allowed him to borrow the most against the money that he had deposited in his account. I will call the banks he chose Bank 1, Bank 2, and Bank 3.

The Execution

Scot walked into Bank 1 and asked to open up a passbook savings account for $1,000. After he opened the account, he thanked the representative and took the passbook home. After about three days, he went back to the bank with his passbook in hand.

He returned to the bank in professional attire and asked to see a loan officer. He chose to dress professionally because he wanted to be taken seriously. He explained to the loan officer that he wished to take out a loan and that he would put up his passbook as collateral. When the loan officer asked his reason for the loan he told him that he was a college student attempting to establish a credit history.

Since Scot was using the money from his savings account as collateral, it did not take long for the loan officer to come back with a decision. The loan officer came back and told Scot that he was allowed to borrow up to 90% of what he had in his savings account ($900). Scot accepted and asked for an installment loan with a one-year repayment schedule. He also asked to be able to make payments on a monthly basis.

Scot wanted everyone in the bank to believe that he was taking out a loan to better his life and that he just wasn't taking out a loan because he needed money. He felt it very important to instill confidence in the loan officer that he would consistently make the monthly payments. Because of his professional dress, his confidence, and the fact that he already had the money in that particular bank, Scot was able to secure the loan and have new information put on his credit report. The loan officer told Scot that his interest rate would be 5%. His monthly payments were $77.05.

Once Scot agreed, the bank froze the $1,000 in his savings account as collateral. The loan officer told Scot that every time he made a payment on his loan, the amount that he paid would be unfrozen. So for example, once he made the first payment, $77.05 would be available. Scot surrendered his passbook to the bank, thanked the loan officer for his time, and left the bank with his $900.

Scot took the $900 from Bank 1 and walked into Bank 2 to open up another passbook savings account. Like before, he waited about three days then walked into the bank with his passbook and asked for a loan. Like before, he made sure to show up dressed in professional attire and appeared very confident.

This time the loan was for $810 (90% of $900) and his monthly payments were $69.27. He then used the $810 and opened up a third savings account at Bank 3. He waited three days and got a third loan for $729 (90% of $810). The monthly payment for this loan was $62.41. So at the end of the first two weeks his financial picture looked something like this.

Bank	Savings Amount	Loan Amount	Payment Amount	Interest Paid
1	$1,000	$900	$77.05	$24.56
2	$900	$810	$69.27	$22.10
3	$810	$729	$62.41	$19.89

His total monthly payments were $208.74. Although this seems like a large number, remember that after his third loan, Scot still had $729 in his pocket. That was enough for the first three monthly payments. With that $729, Scot was able to pay back all the loans in just over 6 months. If you're interested in how he did it, read on!

At this point, he had three loans totaling $2439. He also had $729 in cash from the loan that he just took out at Bank 3. He took the $729 and started to make systematic payments on his loans. He used $77.05 of that $729 and paid his first months payment on the loan at Bank 1. The next day, he went to Bank 2 and Bank 3 and made the first month's payment. At this point, he was about a week ahead on his first payment, two weeks ahead on the second, and three weeks ahead on the third.

He waited two weeks and repeated the same payment process. With this round of payments, he was a full month ahead on all of his monthly payments. With the cash left from his $729, he made a third set of payments a week later. At this point he had about $100 left from his original $729. This is where making those payments early came in handy.

It was time for Scot to go back to the banks and access his savings accounts. Scot remembered that the banks could only hold as much as they needed to secure the amount left on each loan. Because Scot was two months early on all of his payments, he was able to go back to the bank and pull out money from his savings accounts. He used that cash to make the next set of payments on all of his loans.

He continued making payments every two or three weeks until he paid off 6 months on all of his loans. After making 6 months' worth of payments, he went back to each bank and paid off the rest of the loans.

In the end, Scot had three loans taken out in his name totaling just under $2,500. He had a record of making payments for at least six months and also had a record showing that he paid off all of his loans in a timely fashion. Not only that, but he now had three very happy loan officers and three new credit references. That turned out to be very important for him later.

In a little under six months, Scot was able to boost his credit rating as well as gain three new credit references. What a great start for someone 18 years old and a freshman in college.

The Aftermath

In the end, what did this cost Scot? In this example, the interest charged on his loans was 5%. Scot chose banks that gave him, on average, 2% interest so he only ended up paying just above 3% interest. In the end, it cost him just about $15 in interest charges and he still had the original $1,000 that he started with.

Three strong credit references for $15—that is a true bargain of bargains.At this point, Scot had completed part one of his credit-building process. The three references that he acquired helped him a great deal when it came time to get his first set of credit cards. Let's move on to part two to show you how he did it.

Part Two- Getting Secured Credit Cards

This was Scot's first chance to put his credit references to work. Scot knew that he needed to get some credit cards—not because he necessarily needed cash, but because he was looking to build his credit and wanted a convenient way to pay all his monthly bills and make a single payment at the end of the month.

About a week after Scot finished paying off his loans, he went to Bank 1 and asked for an application for a secured Visa credit card. He went home and looked over the application from top to bottom. When he was satisfied that he understood the terms and the fine print, he filled out the application and returned to the bank.

He went to the original loan officer and told him that he was willing to have his $1,000 frozen to secure a credit card with a $1,000 line of credit. Credit cards like this are pretty common and are given to people whether they have good or bad credit. Because Scot was trying to build his credit and had a history of paying back his previous loan early, the bank had no problem offering him a secured credit card with a $1,000 credit limit. Once Scot secured the credit card, he felt that it was time to go out and treat himself to something really nice!

Now Scot knows that credit cards aren't supposed to be used for shopping sprees, but for what he was attempting to do, it served its purpose. Dormant credit cards aren't the best thing to have on a credit report and Scot knew that he wasn't going to use his credit card that often so he wanted to have some activity on the card to show that he did indeed use it. What he did was truly ingenious.

Scot went to his favorite store in his favorite shopping mall. He had been there plenty of times before and knew the store policies very well. Although it was his favorite store, he chose it very carefully. This particular store had a return policy that gave refunds as cash as opposed to giving store credit. See, Scot was not looking to buy something to keep, he was buying something that he wanted to return unopened. Here's why.

When he got his first statement for his new secured credit card, he saw that the transaction that he made was there. More importantly, he saw that the refund for the returned item was interpreted as a payment to his credit card balance. It looks like he paid off the amount in full himself, when in fact he just returned what he bought. So from now on, anyone that pulls up his credit report will see that he made a large purchase ($400) on his credit card and made an on time payment. This was a very large confidence boost for the bank and it helped him when it came time to secure an unsecured credit card.

Part 3- Getting an Unsecured Credit Card

An unsecured credit card is any credit card a banks gives you without holding any of your money as collateral. These types of cards are riskier for both the card holder and the bank. As a result, having and using one effectively will reflect positively on your credit report. Scot knew that just because he was able to get an unsecured credit card didn't mean that he should go get a bunch of them and begin charging away. Instead, he realized that having an unsecured credit card looked good on his credit report; especially when it did not have an outstanding balance.

With the large number of banks that have moved to providing credit cards, it is very hard to not get approved for an unsecured credit card. Many banks will wait out for weeks in tents for freshmen to arrive at colleges across the country and give them an unsecured credit card with nothing more than their college ID! If you are looking to get an unsecured credit card, there are some things that you should consider.

If you are very cerebral about how you manage your money, which credit card you choose to get should not matter. But this is based on a very large presumption: this would mean that you will always pay your entire amount on time and never accrue any interest charges.

I know that realistically there are going to be times in which you are not going to pay the entire bill. I would honestly advise that if you feel that this is the case, you should not make the charge. But there are other times in which emergencies happen and you are not able to pay the full amount. Because this is the case in some situations, you should probably find a credit card that offers the lowest interest rate. Let's talk about some of the things that you should look for when you are choosing a credit card.

When it comes to selecting unsecured credit cards, there are a few major things that you must compare. You should compare interest rates, annual fees, and grace periods. You should shop around to see which has the lowest rate that you can get on the card. If you get anywhere from 12%-15% at this point, you will be in good shape. You must also see if the card has any annual fees.

Some of the better cards like Gold and Platinum cards have higher annual fees. As an incentive, they usually have higher credit limits. For now, you do not need to get one of these cards. You can instead get a regular card that has either a very low fee or no fee at all.

Finally, see what the grace period for finance charges are. Some banks charge you interest the very second that you make the purchase. Others don't charge you for a couple days. Others give you up to a month.

It is important to know when you are being charged interest because it will save you money in the long run when you calculate how much you will have to pay. Finding this information is easy enough. If you do a search on the internet, you will find thousands of different credit offers that promise you every deal under the sun. Make sure you are smart in your selection and only get your credit card from a respectable lender. If you do not feel like going through such a search, you can easily go to a local bank and apply for an unsecured credit card.

At this point in the story, Scot was prepared to free up the original $1,000 that he used to establish his credit profile.

Most adults have not done what he did and he is currently in better shape than most adults and he is now only 20 years old. Scot went back to the bank that he used to get a secured credit card and let the loan officer know that he was now ready to have an unsecured Visa based on his excellent credit history.

He asked if they would be obliged to release the hold on his $1,000 savings. At first the loan officer was hesitant to release the $1,000 but Scot assured him that he would not withdraw the money; he just wanted full access to his account. When the officer still refused to release the funds, as politely as he could, Scot told the officer that he had no other choice than to return the credit card and close the account that he had with them. The loan officer decided to release his funds.

Bringing It All Together

From that point on, the door was wide open to many new forms of credit for Scot. He could get a credit card for frequent flyer miles, a gas card, and even department store cards. I still talk to him and he has a combination of cards and he is very happy with how everything turned out.

Here are some things to think about: The rules of budgeting apply with unsecured cards. You should not charge anything on credit cards that you cannot afford to pay in full at the end of the month. If you question whether or not you will be able to afford it, don't charge it. It is better to not have something now than pay more for it than you were supposed to with interest charges later.

Now, some of you may be asking what score Scot got as a result of doing all that he did and whether or not doing all of that positively affected his credit profile. I can confidently say that Scot's score is sitting comfortably in the 750 range and he is only a junior in college. He has two credit cards and although he doesn't use them regularly, they are still having a very positive impact on his score.

Don't believe me? I will give you proof. I have found a cool tool online that will give you a pretty accurate range of what Scot's credit score was after he finished with the process that I just described. I will walk you through the steps so that you know what values to put in. Are you ready?

Good! Google the phrase FICO Score Estimator. Towards the very top you should see a link to the FICO Score Estimator™ from Bankrate.com. Click on the estimator provided by Bankrate.com. Now click the link that says *Get Started* that's about a quarter of the way down the page. From there it should take you to the questionnaire that will determine the range in which Scot's credit score will be with the information that you put in.

A quick note, Bankrate.com is a well-established consumer website that has a ton of useful information on FICO scores and other great tools about personal finance. I highly recommend you to check out their website as it contains a lot of knowledge that will help in your quest for financial freedom.

Ok, back to the FICO Score Estimator. I will give you the answers that I want you to put into each one of the questions. I will also explain each answer so you know precisely why I am requesting you input that answer. Each answer I give will reflect what was on Scot's credit profile after finishing his credit building process.

Question 1- *How many credit cards do you have?*

Fill in the bubble next to *2-4*. At the end of the process, Scot had two unsecured credit cards. He now has a gas card and a card from his favorite store. Either way, this fits inside the range of 2-4.

Question 1 Follow Up- *How long ago did you get your first credit card?*

Between 6 months and 2 years ago. Scot had been doing this process for 8 months.

Question 2- *How long ago did you get your first loan?*

Between 6 months and 2 years ago. The same logic from question 1-follow up applies here. At this time, Scot got his first 8 months ago.

Question 3- *How many loans or credit cards have you applied for in the last year?*

0. Scot started this process in 2007 which was over a year ago.

Question 4- *How recently have you opened a new line of credit?*

More than six months ago. Scot applied for all of his credit cards more than 6 months ago with his last card applied for 8 months after he started the process.

Question 5- *How many loans and/or credit cards still have a balance?*

0-4. By the time Scott finished the process, he had at least 7 new items on his credit report and three were bank loans. At the conclusion of the process, all three of his loans were paid down. So even if he carried a balance on all four of his cards, the answer would still be *0-4*.

Question 6- *Besides any mortgage loans, what are your total balances on all other loans and credit cards combined?*

Less than $500. Scot doesn't believe in holding onto debt.

Question 7- *When did you last miss a loan or credit card payment?*

I have never missed a payment. Scot never missed a payment during the process. In fact, he was early on every payment that he made.

Question 8- *How many loans and/or credit cards are currently past due?*

0. Once again, all payments were made early not late.

Question 9- *What percent of your total credit card limits do your credit card balances represent?*

0% to 9%. I ask you to input this answer because this process did not call for him to carry a balance on his credit cards. In fact, when he was involved in his credit building process, he greatly discouraged it. If he did have a charge, it was very small and was used for convenience like when shopping online. His outstanding balance never exceeded more than $100. So for that reason, *0% to 9%* is the answer.

Question 10- *Please indicate if you have ever gone through any of the following negative financial events in the last 10 years: bankruptcy, tax lien, foreclosure, repossession, or account referred to collection agency.*

No. His process did the exact opposite.

Once you have submitted the responses, the estimated credit score will be at the top of the page. The score should range from 720-770. Here's your proof.

Conclusion

It just goes to show that it is beneficial to start building your credit as soon as possible. Again, this is just the process that Scot used and it is not to be considered official legal or credit advice. In fact, the process that Scot came up with was borrowed from some of the methods that I use in the Financial Antermology Institute to help my students get their scores into the 770s. Imagine, having a 770 out of 850 just after graduating college!

There are countless adults who have not achieved such a high credit score, ever. This trusted, third party, test from Bankrate.com has shown you more proof than I will ever be able to show you in this book; it has shown you what Scot's credit score is and what almost all of the students of the Financial Antermology Institute credit scores currently are.

Are you excited, yet? I have been excited to share this knowledge with you for a very long time! I feel that building your personal credit is one of the most important things that you will do in your life and it should be taken seriously.

Now let's look at some advanced methods to improve your credit application so that creditors will deem you credit worthy when it is time for you to finance the things that you want. Once you have an understanding of how the application process works, you will have great influence over whether or not you are declined or granted financing. Honestly, when knowing the rules, it will be hard for creditors to not want to give you financing. You are now well on your way to creating a quality lifestyle and you're not even out of college yet! Let's continue.

Review

1. Most colleges teach you very little about establishing a strong financial foundation and credit profile.

2. It is very possible to get bank loans as long as you remain professional and have a purpose.

3. Getting secured credit cards are an easy way to start building a credit history. You can convert them to unsecured cards if you have a consistent "paying on time" history.

4. Bankrate.com is a great online resource

5. Credit cards should be used sparingly and you should never carry high balances for extended periods of time

6. The average credit score of students in the Financial Antermology Institute is 720. Official Antermologists average a score of 775.

Review Questions

1. If you are applying for a credit card, should you go home and read the application fully before you apply?

2. How can you find a list of local banks in your area and learn about their rates?

3. What is the difference between a secured and an unsecured credit card?

Chapter 13

Embellishing Your Credit Application

"If confidence is a plant of slow growth, credit is one which matures much more slowly."
-Benjamin Disraeli

When you are new to credit, every little added advantage helps. Included in this chapter will be a few advanced methods that will help you embellish your credit application and will quickly place you in a position to be more "credit worthy" if you ever need financing.

Your credit profile is not the only thing that creditors look at when they are deciding whether or not they will offer you credit. They look at your monthly income, your debt-to-income ratio, your age, and your assets. These are only a few of the factors in the complex algorithm of credit worthiness. They usually gather all of this information by making you fill out a credit application when applying for financing.

I will take the liberty of showing you several guerilla tactics that will boost those points on your credit application very quickly without you getting a new job, paying down any debt, or adding assets to your credit profile. Let's take a look at the complexities of a credit application.

Nature of Credit Applications

Every bank has an application scoring system that determines whether or not they will accept a credit applicant. And if there were 100,000 banks in your city, I can almost promise that there will be 99,990 different application criteria. Each bank

134

takes different things into account. But even though their needs are very specific, there are some commonalities among all creditors when they are considering granting credit to an applicant.

There are five major factors that creditors deem important:

1. You have a salary of $1,500 or more a month.

2. You have at least 5 years at your current address.

3. You have been employed at your present job for at least two years.

4. You have a "paying on time" credit history.

5. You have a telephone in your name.

Of these five major factors, there isn't one that cannot be manipulated to work in your favor. I will show you how at the conclusion of this section. In the meantime, I want to show you a hypothetical credit application and how the different factors weigh on the individual score:

Preparing to Manage Millions

Credit Scoring System

(This is a sample of the system of a major bank.)

Factors_____ Score_____

1. **Years at job:**

a. Less than one year 0

b. One or two years 1

c. Two to four years 2

d. Four to ten years 3

e. Over ten years 4

2. **Monthly income level**

a. Less than $1,000 0

b. $1,000 to 1,500 1

c. $1,500 to 2,000 2

d. Over $2,000 3

3. **Present obligations past due**

a. Yes 0

b. No 2

4. **Total monthly payments to income after taxes comparison**

a. 50% 0

b. 40 to 49% 1

c. 30 to 39% 2 d. Under 30% 3

5. **Prior loans at any branch bank**

a. No 0

b. Yes, but not closed 0

c. Yes, but closed with two or less eleven-day notices per year 2

6. **Checking account at this bank**

a. None 0

b. Yes, with over five rejected items over the past year 1

c. Yes, with no rejected items In the past year 2

7. **Length at present address**

a. Less than three years 0

b. Three years or more 1

8. **Age of newest automobile**

a. Over one year old 0

b. Less than one year old 1

9. **Savings account**
a. No 0
b. Yes 1

10. **Own real estate**

a. No 0

b. Yes 3

11. **Telephone in own name**

a. No 0

b. Yes 1

12. **Credit references**

a. No 0

b. Yes 1

When you apply for credit, your application is scored and evaluated on the basis of criteria given by the bank's Credit Policy Committee. These criteria vary from bank to bank. Below I have listed the scoring system:

Loan Granted	90-100% points
Loan Granted (unless negative items on credit report)	75-89% points
Risk	50-74% points
Review (With Possible Rejection)	40-49% points
Automatic Rejection	0-39% points

This is only one simplistic version of a credit application. If you are applying for credit in the near future, you may see a credit application that is shorter than this one or you could see one that is considerably longer. It all depends on the lending institution. Most applications will also ask whether you own or lease and give you points based on that. While it is always better to own, most college students do not while they are in school or even when they are right out of school. Lucky for you, there are several ways to lease a residence without living in it or paying for it. Read on and you will learn how to do this.

My goal is to always have you hovering above the 75% level as you are building your credit profile.

Boosting Points on Your Credit Application

There are going to be some areas on your credit application that you are not going to be able to get around. This does not mean that you cannot get around most of them. It is even easier now that you know the major factors that they are looking for. Many people go into an institution asking for credit without knowing what it is going to take to get approved. I do not want to you to be at the same disadvantage.

While there is no fool-proof way of knowing exactly how any individual credit application is weighted, you can maximize the number of points on your credit application by making sure that you satisfy the five major criteria that all major lenders look for. These factors alone count for more than half of the points needed for credit approval. This means that you will be accepted almost all of the time if you can manage to solidify the big five. Let me show you how.

1. You have a salary of $1,500 or more a month.

2.   You have at least 5 years at your current address.

3.   You have been employed at your present job for at least two years.

4. You have a "paying on time" credit history.

5. You have a telephone in your name.

Let's go into detail on how each one of these factors can work in your favor.

Factor 1: *You have a salary of $1,500 or more a month.*

For some students in college, this is possible to obtain. For others, it might not be that easy. $1,500 is not that hard to earn. If you are at a job paying about $32,000 a year, after taxes, you will fall into the category of about $1,500 a month. If you are not there yet, there is no need to fret.

There are some ways to get around it. One way is to have your parents cosign on the financing application. This could satisfy the income requirement. Creditors will also check your parent's credit, though, so hopefully it is not in bad shape.

If you use your parents, you have to ask yourself how you would realistically be able to pay for what you are attempting to finance. Depending on the amount of money you are attempting to get, some companies will be a bit more lenient with their standards. If you are trying to purchase a big-ticket item like a house or a car, $1,500 is the absolute minimum amount that you should make every month.

If you are attempting to finance a house though, $1,500 is the minimum that you should be making every two weeks! Honestly, I am not in the business of getting you into financial trouble. Although Financial Antermologists are not against financing, we are absolutely against financing something if you can't comfortably afford it. If you have to resort to trickery to be able to (or claim to) afford the minimum amount of money you should make every month for financing, chances are you should wait until you do make that much. Trust us—it will save you a lot of pain in the long run.

Factor 2- You Have at Least 5 Years at Your Current Address

If you are in college, chances are, you still use your parent's house as your primary residence. If you do, that is great;

you have been living at that place your entire life. Placing your home address on the application will easily satisfy the minimum requirement for years living in a residence. Of course, there is much more that goes into how long you have been living at a residence. This is where knowing about leases is very important.

Did you know that you can have a lease that says that you are leasing out your home and you are doing nothing more than storing stuff in your room while you are at school? Yes, you can have your parents draft up a lease and have it notarized to prove that you are currently leasing your room. Now realistically, you shouldn't have to pay your parents a dime, but you have a slip of paper telling creditors that you are currently leasing a residence. For most applications that will boost the points. You will be able to use this until you are able to either lease your own place or buy your first property.

Factor 3- You Have Been Employed at Your Current Job at Least Two Years.

If you have worked at your job for that long, then great. As college students, for the most part, having a job for two years is just not a reality. You are oftentimes home during the summer and cannot realistically say that you have worked at your current job for two years. What you can do, though, is ask your manager for help. If you have worked at a place for two years but take summers off, you can ask the manager to tell creditors that. Most creditors will count that as you working for two years at your current job.

If you haven't been working at your job for two years, depending on what you're financing, the creditor could be quite lenient. I have known many students fresh out of college with 0 months on the job who have been financed for an automobile. I have known students with no job at all who have gotten financing for a new laptop. It is very possible to achieve financing for certain items without being on a job for two years or more. The most important thing that a creditor wants to know is whether or not they are going to get paid back If you can demonstrate that then you will be more than alright.

I have known individuals to use some pretty shady tactics to get around how long they have been at their current jobs. Again, I do not advise you that use any shady tactics for the sake of getting financing. Anything immoral or unlawful will almost always surface and it will definitely damage your credibility, even if it surfaces ten years later. If you have learned nothing else from politicians, I am sure you have learned that!

Factor 4- You Have a Paying-on-Time Credit History

If you have not made any mistakes during your college years and have begun to start building your credit, then you should be fine. If you feel that your credit may need some additional work, consider joining the Financial Antermology Institute. I have a proven system (ask Scot!) that can get your credit into the 700's in less than the time it will take you to complete a school year.

Note that a paying on-time-credit history only accounts for about 20-30% of the points needed to be granted credit. I want you to have a strong credit profile so that you will consistently receive this 30% and only have to worry about the other 45%. But having a strong credit profile makes getting that 45% even easier, believe me. Let's move on to the final factor.

Factor 5- You Have a Telephone in Your Name

This is also another category to receive the maximum amount of points easily. I just have one word to point you in the right direction: Vonage. This internet phone service has completely revolutionized phone service around the globe. They have gotten so good that they are now competing with the cellular phone industry. And here's the reason.

Most cellular phone bills start at about $50 a month after taxes. Some are more than $100 a month! And let's not even mention text messaging fees, overage charges, and roaming. All together, the cellular phone industry easily gets rich by charging extra fees to the average consumer. Vonage, on the other hand, tries a different approach.

Vonage Internet Phone Service offers you unlimited EVERYTHING. This means unlimited incoming and outgoing minutes, free nationwide long distance, free equipment, free voice mail system, free call waiting, free call forwarding, free caller id, free free free free free!

And all of this comes to you at a whopping $24.99 a month. With taxes, you pay a grand total of $27.82. Does that sound anything close to the price of your cellular phone bill? I didn't think so. On top of all that, Vonage also offers a wireless phone that allows you to pick up a signal in Wi-Fi areas. This means that you can take your room phone anywhere on campus that has a wireless signal and make free phone calls. This, my friends, is what we like to call a room phone on steroids!

To sweeten the deal, Vonage has a referral program that is optimal for the college student. I say this because it allows you to reach out to people in your network and simply recommend Vonage to your friends. When you get them to sign up, they receive their first month free as an added bonus. You, on the other hand, receive more than that.

You receive a credit to your account that will last you just about two months. So imagine this, you get referred to Vonage and receive your first month free. Now you have thirty days to refer two friends to sign up at Vonage. When you do, you will have your first five months free. To put it another way, your entire first semester is free!

If you repeat this process next semester with just two more friends, you have your second semester free, also. Not a bad way to get a free phone is it? The best part is your friends can do it, too. So you can sell them on accepting your referral by helping them do the same thing that you are doing. Believe me, it makes convincing them a LOT easier.

Let me show you how this will allow you to save on your wireless bill. Once you have your Vonage phone, you will notice that you will use your cell phone half as often. This prevents overage charges. Vonage also allows text messages to your landline. Soon you will see that you only use your cell phone when you are off campus. This means that you can downgrade your plan, which saves you even more money. I guess their slogan is true after all: Vonage *Is* the way to go.

You can use your Vonage phone for a business line as well. You can add an additional line for free and just pay the $24.99 a month. That would mean that you would have a personal and business/fax line with unlimited everything for less than you probably pay now for your current cell phone bill. This strategy is a major steal if you ask me and I want you to benefit from every steal that I know.

Conclusion

I have just shown you how to get half the required points on most credit applications and you really haven't put in too much effort yourself. You have not worked any additional hours or asked your boss for a raise that you knew you were not going to get. Getting the other 25% depends on the specific questions on the credit application and really cannot be answered here. Just remember that the lower debt-to-income ratio you have the better off you are going to be. Some applications ask specific questions concerning whether or not your home is furnished. And believe it or not, you get more points if your home is unfurnished.

If you find yourself needing to make more money in order to get financed for something, it may be your first indication that you are not living within your means. You should never use the tools in this chapter to get financing for something that you can't afford in the first place. This chapter was included because I wanted to make sure that you are guaranteed financing for something that you have already made a plan for and you know that you can afford.

If you use the information in this chapter to finance something that you cannot afford, you may very well end up in a situation where you are in over your head in finance charges and your entire budgeting plan and financial future will suffer as a consequence. Let's make sure that never happens. Please be very deliberate about what you choose to finance.

Review

1. Every bank has different credit criteria.

2. If you can handle the big five, chances are you won't be declined for a loan.

3. It is never ok to lie on your credit application or use deceitful tactics to get financing.

4. Vonage is the way to go!

Review Questions

1. What are the big five on a credit application?

2. What are some ways to give your credit application an extra boost?

3. What should you do if you can't satisfy the minimum monthly income requirements?

4. What could you do if you have not been working at your job for two years?

Chapter 14

Winning the Credit Card Game

"Remember That Credit is Money."
-Benjamin Franklin

When you are in college, they come in the mail every day. They sit waiting for you when you return home. They are even in your email inboxes. Credit card offers are everywhere! And every day, there is a new great deal that is trying its best to give you what appears to be free money.

No Interest for the first year! No Annual Fees! 0% APR! There isn't a day that goes by that you are not bombarded with a number of offers that promise you everything in the world. Most of these companies don't even care about whether or not you have good credit. They just want to put a card in your hand so that they can start making money from interest. Before you make a decision to get a credit card, there are some things you need to consider.

Your first question when considering whether or not to get a credit card is what you need it for! Credit cards are a convenient way to pay your bills and buy items in a store without having to carry large amounts of cash on you. This should be the ONLY reason that you have a credit card. They should not be used for cash advances or for temporary loans. The interest that you will have to pay for such a loan will always be far more than you ever should pay per dollar. Now the question may arise:

"If I am only using a credit card as a convenient way to pay bills or make purchases, why don't I just use a debit card?"

The answer is simple: debit cards do not show up on your credit report. If you use a credit card like you use your debit card, by only spending the money that you have in your bank account, your everyday debit transactions will help your credit score if you put them on your credit card. You will not reap the same benefits from using your debit card as you would your credit card. You just have to make sure that you only charge what you can afford.

Also, debit cards do not carry the same identity theft protection that most credit cards do. This is very important as identity theft is the fastest growing crime in the world. If you use your credit card online and someone snatches your identity, your credit card company will oftentimes not hold you responsible for the ID theft transactions. Debit cards, on the other hand, don't carry such protection. If an ID thief gets access to your debit card and completely cleans out your bank account, most times your bank will not replace what was stolen. So next time you are doing your online shopping, think wisely about whether you are going to use your debit or your credit card.

Your second question to ask when deciding whether or not you will get a credit card is what you want your limit to be. At this point in your life, you really do not need a credit card with a high limit. This will only tempt you to make a budgeting mistake and not live within your means. You have to choose an amount that you know you will be able to pay off, even when times are hard. A good number to select is the amount that you have in your savings and emergency fund combined.

For example, let's say that you have a combined total of $1,000 in your savings and emergency accounts. I would advise you to set your credit limit to $750. This way, if you ever ran into trouble and did not have the money to pay the bill off entirely, you will have more than enough to cover it in your bank account. This will save you from unwanted interest charges, as well as any potential blemishes that could appear in your credit profile.

A third question that you must consider when thinking about whether or not to get a credit card is "Why does this company want me so bad?" It is this question that will save you thousands of dollars! Most credit card

Most credit card companies don't care about you – they care about profits.

companies don't care who you are, how much money you make, or what school you go to. All they care about is profits. Statistically, a majority of college students leave college with close to $3,000 in debt. This number shows that students are not paying off their credit card bills completely every month.

This means a very hefty sum that credit card companies make off interest from offering credit cards to students. And for that reason, they sell you on their offer that seems too good to be true.   You know the saying; if something appears too good to be true, it probably is. This could not be truer for credit card offers. I'm going to stress this point again—it is imperative that you realize this truth.

They will send you information in the mail, making it appear that all the people that work in their company are a family. And they sell you even more by telling you that they want you to be a part of their family. They are very deliberate about offering you all kinds of perks for joining the family. They won't rest until you believe that they have your best interest at heart.

This is a fantasy. Family members wouldn't charge you an astronomical amount of interest if you do not pay them back on time. They would not charge you late fees. They would not include hidden charges in the temporary loan that they would give you. And they would not slander your name publicly (on your credit report) if you are a couple days late on paying them back. It honestly isn't worth it to have a credit card from some of the companies that send you offers in the mail.

Let's take a little time to talk about the vast amount of ways that credit card companies take advantage of the average card holder. Some of this information will shock you. When I learned this information, I immediately wanted to cut up my credit cards. I have since changed my mind. I now know that credit cards are positive for your credit report when you are responsible with them.

I now only charge small amounts for items that I already have the money for. I also use it to make larger purchases so that I do not have to carry cash around. When I get home at the end of the day, I usually send a check to the credit card company to pay for the item I bought earlier that day. If there was something large that I didn't have the money for, I found another way to pay for it.

Annual vs. Effective Interest Rates

This is probably one of the best kept secrets of credit card companies. I have found that some people know the difference between these two concepts; very few of them have been college students. And you are the person who needs to know this the most so I have included it in this book.

A credit card's annual rate (APR) is the rate that you get on the sheet of paper that comes with your credit card offer or the actual credit card. Most credit card companies entice their customers with a low introductory APR. Don't pay attention to that one. We are looking for the APR that comes once the introductory period is over. The APR for credit cards can range anywhere from 10-40% with an average of about 19-25% for college students. This means that on average, if you charge $1,000 on your credit card and make payments instead of paying off the entire amount, you will pay $190-$220 in interest a year. Yikes!

Remember back to chapter 12 where Scot got three loans? Do you remember the total amount of interest that was paid on the $1,000 loan that he took out? That's right; it was less than $30! The high amount that you must pay is not the worst part of the percentage rate of credit cards. Believe it or not, you always will end up paying more than the annual percentage rate on credit cards. Let me introduce you to the concept of an effective percentage rate.

Unlike the annual percentage rate, which is given to you by the credit card company; the effective percentage rate is determined by how often the interest is compounded. Put plainly, the effective interest rate is the

Go to www.copocket.co for a free effective interest rate calculator.

actual rate you pay a year on the card. This is where the policy of the credit card issuer is very important. There are some credit card companies that won't charge interest for 30 days, while others will charge interest from the moment of purchase. You must know how often they charge interest because this will determine how much you will actually pay for the charge on the credit card.

Let me give you an example for clarity. Let's say you have a credit card with an APR of 19% that is compounded monthly. Because the interest is compounded monthly instead of yearly, every month, you are paying interest on the 19% interest you already owe. As a result, you will not pay 19%; you will pay 21% annually. 21% is your annual effective rate, or the interest you will actually have to pay. If the company compounds daily, the effective percentage rate will be higher!

So depending on how often the credit card company compounds interest, you will pay anywhere from 19%-23% annually. By law, they have to tell you the annual percentage rate, and they must tell you how often they compound interest. They are not required, however, to put the information together and tell you the effective percentage rate. If you do not take the time to calculate it on your own, you will never know.

Special Introductory Offers

Every great credit card offer has to provide something that no other credit card does. Unfortunately, bad credit card offers do the same. The only difference is great credit card companies do it to help and bad credit card companies do it to lure you in for profits. You must learn to be able to tell the difference between the two if you want to win the credit card game.

When looking for a good credit card offer, read the fine print that comes with the offer. Call the company and see how accessible a customer service representative is. Come up with some questions you have about the materials and the offer and ask them to clarify. Ask them how long their introductory offer lasts and what the terms will be once the offer is over. Ask them about annual fees. Ask them everything that you want until you are satisfied. If at any point during the conversation you are not happy with any of their answers, you have the freedom to walk away from the offer altogether.

You can also choose not to play the game at all. I am not

saying that all credit cards are bad. In previous chapters, I went over several methods to get a credit card that will work in your favor. I am just saying that most credit card offers that come in the mail should go straight in the shredder; they will get you in more trouble than they will help you. I have already shown you the safe and effective way to get a credit card. These cards, along with all that you have learned about budgeting, will take you a long way while you are developing your credit. But I digress.

Back to credit card offers. We must remember the term that is used with all of the introductory credit card offers: introductory! There is a finite amount of time in which you will receive 0% APR or no annual fees. It is important to know what the case will be once the introductory period is over. I'm sure it will be a pleasant surprise to know that once your 0%APR period ends, yourAPR is now 25%! It has happened to the best of us; let's make sure that it doesn't happen to you.

Also, the introductory offers usually have strict guidelines while they are in effect. What do you think will happen if you are ever late on a payment? You got it: that introductory offer is taken away from you. This will happen even if your payment is a couple days late. Now you are stuck with a credit card that has no competitive advantage over any of the other credit cards that you had to choose from. And in the meantime, the credit card company is in a position to charge you a high interest rate, along with a late fee. It is a win-win for them.

Either they get a new customer who will pay their bills on time or they have a new customer who will continue to give them money via late fees and interest payments. The benefits for you don't outweigh the costs. It is my professional opinion that you should stay away from these kinds of credit card offers.

Conclusion

I know these credit cards are usually easy to get. I also know that they look very attractive when they come in the mail. But I have already shown you several ways in which to get a credit card that is currently working to your advantage and not the other way around. So, let's continue using the safe credit cards and building on the current relationships that you are building with the banks that you have them with. This will help you greatly down the line when you are attempting to get larger loans for things like a car or your first home

Review

1. Most credit card offers in the mail are a waste of time.

2. It is smart to use a credit card rather than a debit card when shopping online.

3. Identity Theft is the fastest growing crime in the world.

4. Credit cards are not your friend.

5. Annual interest rates are on credit card offers; the effective interest rate is what you actually pay.

6. Pay attention to the condition of introductory credit card rates.

Review Questions

1. What are the advantages to using credit cards when doing your online shopping?

2. What is the difference between an annual and effective interest rate?

3. Why is it important to pay attention to introductory credit card offers?

Chapter 15

Maintaining Good Credit After College

"Only the educated are free."
-Epictetus

With everything that has been mapped out in this book, you should be well on your way to financial freedom. Of course, when it comes to finances, credit, and budgeting, no one will ever learn everything that there is to know. I have researched these topics for years and still learn something new every day. With changes in technology and improvements to the system itself, there is always something new to learn and apply to your life.

In just reading and applying the concepts included in this book, you are in great shape financially. As you leave college with your great credit score, your superb credit profile, and your wealth of knowledge on credit and budgeting, maintaining great credit after college is a personal choice. This program will give you a 4.0 personal finance GPA. It is your job to keep that grade point average high. I know you can do it; just finishing this book shows me you have what it takes. I understand that even when armed with the knowledge to becoming financially free, it is helpful to have someone there to help if you ever have any questions. This way, instead of using trial and error, which could lead to some costly mistakes, you can ask someone who has done it right the first time.

I wrote this book because I want you to get it right the first time and now I have taken my commitment to your success one step further. Recently, my company, The Financial Antermology Institute, launched a new website (www.copocket.co) that has revolutionized the way college students approach credit and debt. My new site hosts a community of college students just like you who are mastering the art of achieving financial freedom. All of the blogs, message boards, and FAQ forums are monitored by my dedicated staff to quickly help you. And when you become a member of our online community, you even get a free consultation with me! Yes, I will personally contact you and answer any specific questions you have about your journey to financial freedom.

My site includes a wealth of new knowledge on budgeting and credit. In addition to the large online community, The CoPocket site will soon include 36 additional chapters covering everything from how credit card interest is calculated to what to do when it is time to purchase your first car or home. The site also includes practical tools to help you become a credit and budgeting master.

Do you need help applying what is in this book? If so, my team and I at CoPocket have a service called the Advanced Credit Accelerator that helps you build your credit score to 720 or higher in 6 months of less. We have established all the banking relationships that you will need to complete the credit building process for you. This is just one of the many exciting benefits of joining the CoPocket community.

Before I go, I would like to say something. This final chapter serves as a thank you from me to you; I end my seminars the same way. Whenever I tell people thank you at the close of a presentation, there is usually one person that makes this comment: *"You have taught us so much, shouldn't we be the ones thanking you?"*

While I gladly accept acknowledgement for the passion that I have for helping people, I have a greater passion for the

actual people who want to be helped.
My response to that question is this.

"Yes, you can thank me, but I will never ask to be thanked. I thank you because you value the information that I give out. Like me, you realize that there is something seriously wrong with the system that we live in and you are taking steps to better yourself, thus taking power away from the system.

With every person that makes a commitment to their financial future, my passion for teaching people how to free themselves from the slavery of debt gets rejuvenated. This is not my job…it is my life's work. So thank you.

Thank you for helping me make a difference, one person at a time. Thank you for believing that there is a better way. And most of all, thank you for asking the question "who says that our current conception of our financial future has to remain that way?"

Thank you for taking the time to read this book. I hope that I have helped in your quest toward financial freedom and that you achieve every dream that you dream for yourself.